A History of the Sidecar
TT Races, 1923–2023

A History of the Sidecar TT Races, 1923–2023

Matthew Richardson

AN IMPRINT OF PEN & SWORD BOOKS LTD.
YORKSHIRE – PHILADELPHIA

First published in Great Britain in 2024 by
Pen and Sword Transport
An imprint of
Pen & Sword Books Ltd.
Yorkshire - Philadelphia

Copyright © Matthew Richardson, 2024

ISBN 9781399044547

The right of Matthew Richardson to be identified as author of this work has been asserted by him in accordance with the Copyright, Designs and Patents Act 1988.

A CIP catalogue record for this book is available from the British Library.

All rights reserved. No part of this book may be reproduced or transmitted in any form or by any means, electronic or mechanical including photocopying, recording or by any information storage and retrieval system, without permission from the Publisher in writing.

Typeset in INDIA by IMPEC eSolutions
Printed and bound in the UK on paper from a sustainable source by
CPI Group (UK) Ltd., Croydon. CR0 4YY.

Pen & Sword Books Ltd. incorporates the imprints of Pen & Sword Books: After the Battle, Archaeology, Atlas, Aviation, Battleground, Discovery, Family History, History, Maritime, Military, Politics, Select, Transport, True Crime, Fiction, Frontline Books, Leo Cooper, Praetorian Press, Seaforth Publishing, Wharncliffe and White Owl.

For a complete list of Pen & Sword titles please contact:

PEN & SWORD BOOKS LIMITED
George House, Beevor Street, Off Pontefract Road,
Hoyle Mill, Barnsley, South Yorkshire, England, S71 1HN
E-mail: enquiries@pen-and-sword.co.uk
Website: www.pen-and-sword.co.uk

or

PEN AND SWORD BOOKS
1950 Lawrence Rd, Havertown, PA 19083, USA
E-mail: Uspen-and-sword@casematepublishers.com
Website: www.penandswordbooks.com

Contents

Acknowledgments	vii
Introduction	xi
Chapter 1 Pioneer Days	1
Chapter 2 The Return	16
Chapter 3 German Domination	38
Chapter 4 Dawn of Japan	82
Chapter 5 Manx Monopoly	143
Chapter 6 Age of the Champions	182
Epilogue – The Future	204
Notes	206
Bibliography	212
Index	213

Acknowledgments

This book is the product of many years of interest and research into the history of sidecar racing at the Isle of Man TT races. During those years I have been fortunate enough to have met, spoken to and learned from many people whose knowledge of sidecar racing far eclipses my own. On the Isle of Man I must thank Helen Gibson, who has never stinted in sharing knowledge and contacts from her many years of experience in the sidecar world. It was Helen who introduced me to the late great Stan Dibben, one of the unsung heroes of British motorsport. Also on the Isle of Man, Dave Molyneux allowed me access to his photographs and memories of three decades of success at the TT. It is fair to say that Dave is as much of an authority on the history of sidecar racing as he is an exponent of the current racing situation. I learned a tremendous amount from him when we worked together on his memoir *The Racer's Edge* in 2010 and I remain indebted to him. Ben and Tom Birchall were kind enough to help me with information and insights, and I thank them warmly. Kenny Arthur provided me with invaluable details of his racing partnership with George O'Dell.

In Germany, Lothar Mildebrath helped me enormously with the heritage of BMW in racing and I am grateful to him for allowing me a copy from his limited print run of the book *Münchener Meistermacher Maschinen*. Likewise, former World Champion Max Deubel was generous with his time and assistance, as was Josef Ried, who for many years was a mechanic for another BMW ace, Georg Auerbacher. Also in Germany, Ruth Standfuss of the BMW historical archive helped me to locate the 1955 BMW poster that appears herein; I gratefully acknowledge BMW Group Classic as the source of this image. On the Isle of Man, Vanda Murray provided some marvellous insights into her father's career as one of the TT's first sidecar passengers, and I thank her sincerely. John Watterson at Isle of Man Newspapers also helped with photographs, for which I am extremely grateful. I especially wish to mention John Chisnall and Anthony Davis, who very kindly allowed me to quote from their joint memoir *And the Wheels Went Round*. To anyone who has not yet seen this book, I thoroughly recommend it. John began his career as a sidecar passenger in 1957 and the book is a wonderful collection of anecdotes from the Golden Age of racing.

Again I am deeply indebted to the late Ken Sprayson for the use of his highly evocative images from the 1960s and 1970s. Ken always seemed to be in the right spot to capture an historic moment, and was always willing to share his pictures with me. His atmospheric TT photographs have enhanced a number of projects on which I have worked over the years. Wendy Thirkettle and Jude Dicken assisted me with several images from the Manx National Heritage archive, for which I am grateful. Others who contributed photographs and whom I thank warmly include Mark Dibben, Julie Hanks-Elliott, Kirsty and June Saville, and J.A. Ranscombe of Ranscombe

Brothers Photographic. John Newton read the early draft, and helped me to avoid several pitfalls, for which I thank him. Likewise my thanks also go to Simon Crellin at the Isle of Man Government Motorsport Office for assistance with use of the TT trademark. Naturally any errors of fact or interpretation are my own; for an author, it is also lamentably easy to cause offence by omission. To anyone who for reasons of space I was not able to mention, I extend my sincere apologies.

Matthew Richardson
Douglas, Isle of Man, 2024

Introduction

Sidecar racing is often thought of as the Cinderella of motorsports. At UK circuits in the 1970s it was customary to send the three-wheelers out at the end of the day's racing as it was believed that they would drop oil on the track. To the dismay of sidecar racers this was also usually just as most of the fans were going home.

Sidecar competitors also traditionally find it difficult to attract sponsorship from the major motorcycle manufacturers. Unlike solo racing, success on the track does not translate easily and directly into increased showroom sales. Honda after all do not make and retail sidecar outfits as part of their range on offer to the high street customer.

Yet perhaps manufacturers should pay more attention to sidecar successes, because the engine in a sidecar outfit has to undertake twice the workload of that in a solo, and has to carry the weight of two bodies. Also, unlike that of a solo machine, in a sidecar the throttle is pinned wide open for most of the distance of the race.

In no other form of motorsport do two riders have to work so closely together, and the class is particularly noted for the personalities that it attracts – individuals of differing outlooks but who are often united by a common thread of being technically creative innovators.

The sidecar races at the TT are particularly special. Most short circuits, certainly in the United Kingdom, are constructed at former airfields and thus are generally fairly level. No other course includes the gradients of the Isle of Man's Mountain circuit, and no other tests machines – and riders – to their absolute limits. When World Championship motorcycle racing was born in 1949, sidecars and solos enjoyed equal precedence and this was true certainly through the 1960s, and even into the 1970s. Since then, the birth of World Superbikes and MotoGP have tended to push sidecar racing down the pecking order at international level. Only the sidecar race at the TT has really maintained its status. When Grand Prix racers started to boycott the solo TT races in the early 1970s, the sidecar World Championship contenders stayed loyal, and even when the TT lost Grand Prix status, World Champions continued to support it. This has continued into the twenty-first century and today the sidecar races at the TT are regarded by many in the sport as even bigger and more prestigious than the World Championship.

Chapter 1

Pioneer Days

The first sidecar race at the TT was run in 1923, and immediately it established itself as one of the most exciting classes at the meeting, indeed the *Isle of Man Times* described that first event as 'the most thrilling race in the world'. For sheer spectacle, little can beat sidecar racing and right from those early days it was obvious that to be successful both teamwork and mutual trust between rider and passenger were essential.

Sidecars were a popular early form of family transport, and by simply bolting the wheeled car onto a standard motorcycle, the Edwardian rider could immediately add versatility to his machine, enabling him to transport additional passengers or extra goods. Motorcycle and sidecar combinations had seen a great deal of service during the First World War, bringing them to wider attention, and it was at the third post-war meeting that a race for these outfits first appeared on the TT programme. It has sometimes been stated that the discontinuing of these races was one of the greatest missed opportunities in the history of the TT. Given more time the class could have raised the social status of the motorcycle and sidecar, introduced them to a wider audience, and increased their commercial viability, but it was not to be.

The first race was to be run over three laps of the Mountain Course, on the Wednesday afternoon of Race Week, immediately after the Lightweight TT. One of the pioneers of the event was 'Fast Freddie' Dixon (born Frederick William Dixon, on 21 April 1892 at 31 Alliance Street, Stockton-on-Tees). Freddie left school at the age of 13 and went to work in a cycle shop, soon moving to Kit McAdam's Garage in Yarm Lane as an apprentice mechanic. He acquired his first motorcycle in 1909 and within a year was competing in speed and hill climb events in and around Stockton-on-Tees. In 1912, at the age of 19, he competed in the Isle of Man TT races for the first time on a Cleveland Precision motorcycle, but sadly the machine was not up to the challenge and in the Senior he was forced to retire. However, Freddie's disillusionment with this standard 'off the shelf' machine, and its lack of suitability for the task in hand, inspired his passion for tinkering with and improving standard or basic models.

During the First World War, Freddie spent four years in the Royal Army Service Corps (RASC) rising to the rank of staff sergeant. On returning to civilian life he went into business for himself at Park Garage on Linthorpe Road, Middlesbrough, though he continued to compete in motorcycle races, with placings in various race categories throughout the 1920s. He continued to persevere with the Indian brand in the solo races during those early post-war years at the TT, but it was aboard a 500cc Douglas that he chose to compete in that first sidecar race. Dixon wrote later:

> My win in the 1923 Sidecar TT rather stands out in my memory as a kind of joke with a lucky break in it. Having arranged to ride a Douglas outfit in this race I thought

I had better get down to the factory in Bristol to see what sort of a job was being prepared. I found they were busy making up a job with a leaning body and I didn't much care for it. As there was only about a week before we must leave for the Island, I was quite a bit worried, and after one or two sleepless nights, I dreamt of that comic thing – the 'banking sidecar'.

It seemed a hopeless proposition to get one made up in time, but I thought 'nothing venture – nothing gain [sic]', and promptly turned my sex appeal on to Bill Bailey, who was in charge at the time. He laughed when I mooted the idea of getting one through in time, but I eventually persuaded him that it might be done and he placed the whole resources of the factory at my disposal.

There was no time for drawings so I did a quick bit of chalking on the Experimental Shop floor, and with a few willing helpers, and not bothering about sleep, we knocked up a complete sidecar with an all-metal body having a rolling seat, as used by some oarsmen. Nothing needed modification, and my first passenger – the one and only Alec Bennett – was enthusiastic at the tricks we could get up to.[1]

Dixon's design was simplicity itself, and it combined tremendous strength with the advantage that it did not produce a fixed bank, but one that could be adjusted by the passenger. It is interesting to note that it took Dixon only ten days to build up his TT-winning frame, after the idea came to him. It is clear that nothing particularly complicated was used, and the design was quickly patented by Dixon and the chief engineer at Douglas, S.L. Bailey, with a view to potentially turning it into a commercial proposition.

The principle did not rely upon any swivelling joints, ball joints, universal joints, or similar devices. Dixon's plan was simply to raise and lower the sidecar wheel. That is to say, if he raised the sidecar wheel spindle, it meant that the outfit naturally dropped towards the nearside, for of course the outfit would not balance with the wheel in the air! As it dropped it canted over, and so the crew obtained a natural banked angle, the sidecar and driving wheels being parallel but canted over into a degree determined by the amount of lift given to the sidecar wheel. Similarly, if the sidecar wheel bearing were dropped, the frame was raised, and so the outfit tended to lean towards the offside, the position, of course, required for turning to the right. It is perhaps not easy to make the design clearly understood in words, but it may help to emphasise the simplicity of the mechanism to state that the only extra moving part on the outfit was the arm on which the sidecar wheel was mounted.

Dixon's frame, as well as being simple, was also immensely strong. It was attached to his machine at three points, and the chassis was triangulated. All the connections were at footrest level, there being no saddle seat tie rod or connection below the head. Two of the connections were large diameter and passed right through the duplex Douglas frame. The third transverse member was made hollow and formed the axle of the sidecar wheel. On it rotated a 7in arm webbed for strength and carrying the sidecar wheel spindle. Passing through the hollow axle was a control rod, coupled with a lever arranged between the sidecar body and the machine. A second lever also mounted on this rod occupied a similar position on the nearside of the body. These levers raised or lowered the sidecar wheel, according to whether they were pushed forward or backwards, and two were provided to enable the passenger to have control of the banking apparatus whether he were leaning over the back wheel of the machine or over the sidecar wheel.

It required a considerable amount of strength to raise or lower the sidecar fame and the passenger's own weight by means of these levers, so Dixon arranged a spring balance effect on them to make their operation a good deal easier. Rachets and pawls made it possible for the levers to be locked in any suitable position, press-knobs being provided to release the pawls just as is common on motorcar handbrake levers.

A rod passing through the hollow axle operated the sidecar brake. The body was made of aluminium, sand blasted on its upper surface to prevent sun glare, and another typical 'Dixonish' gadget was a sliding seat for the passenger. The seat itself and its back were arranged on rollers, something after the manner of a seat in a rowing boat. The passenger could at will slide his body forward in the sidecar and thus move the back rest into a horizontal position so that he could lie flat, or by sliding backwards he could raise the back of the seat to enable him to adopt a normal sitting position, in which attitude he was better able to control the banking levers.

Dixon was one of the most careful mechanics who ever rode in a TT race. He did nearly all his work himself, and trusted nobody with his machines. Most motorcyclists of the day knew his little fads such as a back rest on his saddle, footboards and so forth, but it is not generally known that he also employed two twist grip controls, one on each end of the handlebars, on his sidecar machine, so that he could work his throttle when both hands were on the left-hand bar, whilst he was cornering to the left. Apart from throttle controls, he had a horror of wire cables and wherever possible he would employ rods. For instance, his sidecar brake was rod operated, so were the ignition controls, extra air levers, oil pumps and anything else that needed working, and could be operated without the aid of a wire cable.

Freddie had made several other modifications to the motorcycle itself, one of which was to the oiling, which originally was a 'Total Loss' system. It was operated by means of a hand pump (with a lever on the right handlebar) contained in the oil tank below the engine. This could easily flood the engine with oil, so Freddie cut a large hole about an inch in diameter in both crankcase and tank, sealed the gap with a rubber ring, and let the oil drain back to the tank. Large breathers were added to cope with crankcase compression. It is not generally known that there was also an ingenious telltale metering valve for the oil supply. This was in the petrol tank near the front. When the spring-loaded pump was delivering, the telltale knob lifted. Rotating the knob brought a succession of different-size holes into line with the outlet, ranging from almost nil to full bore. The attention to detail in even the smallest areas was a credit to Dixon's engineering skill. No bolt was used where a tube and split pin could serve the same purpose, all bolts where it was permissible were hollow, all frame lugs were scarfed and tapered to the limit. To save weight, mudguards were made of aluminium, wheel rims were made of special alloy that made them very light, and extensive use of special steel alloys even permitted the rear wheel spindle to be 'waisted' down to ⅜in between threaded portions. Freddie takes up the story once again:

> We landed in the Isle of Man feeling very happy, but had a nasty shock when the scrutineers put the bar up and said we could not use such a dangerous contraption, and during the early practice period we had to have the works locked in the rigid position. However, my pleading availed, and we were allowed to use the gadget for one lap under close observation at different parts of the course. The job worked fine, and we carved quite a chunk off the lap record with my passenger, young Walter Denny, sitting in a perfectly normal manner.[2]

In fact, Dixon set the lap record in practice and was the hot favourite to win the race, ahead of close rival Graham Walker (father of commentator Murray Walker), who was riding a 588cc Norton outfit. Walker was no slouch himself when it came to mechanical innovation, and he actually designed the Hughes sidecar that he used in the race specifically for the purpose. Because 'Pa' Norton (owner of the company) was on an economy drive, he had cut the works entries that year down to just two solos. Even though he was the competition manager at Norton at the time, Walker was forced to pay his own expenses. To raise funds he sold his sidecar design to the Hughes brothers, a small Birmingham firm of sidecar builders, for a sum of around £50, a free sidecar, and his TT entry fee.

Walker's design would turn out to be one of the few that could withstand the rigours of racing on the Mountain Course at over 50mph, contending with potholes and loose stones along the way, and he would be rewarded with second place in the coming race. Dixon continues his account thus:

> The day of the race came with things looking very rosy and off we went. We very quickly passed those who had started before us. As it appeared we had so much in hand, I eased up considerably, and Denny and I entertained each other up the Mountain singing 'We Won't be Home Till Morning'.
>
> A shock was coming for I had forgotten those behind, and suddenly there was a nasty scream and Harry Langman passed us. Mental calculation told me that we would really have to get our skates on now. Up went the wick and I soon repassed him, not knowing whether he would need to stop for fuel, as we must do. I got that job over, and was just pushing off, when Harry came chasing through. He led me through Braddan Bridge, and we arrived there some two seconds later to find him upside down and sliding all over the place. We missed him, but I don't know to this day how it was done.
>
> Breathing a sigh of relief, I kept the steam on, thinking there might be others I had miscalculated. More trouble was brewing, for as we took Hillberry on this – the last – lap, at somewhat hectic speed, the inner duplex frame tube suddenly snapped. The handlebar jamming on the body stopped a total collapse, but it was only by wangling

the banking lever that we were able to hobble home and see the welcome chequered flag.[3]

They won the race by covering the three laps in two hours, seven minutes and forty-eight seconds, giving an average speed of 53.15mph, winning comfortably over Graham Walker and George Tucker. Walker's rear brake (just a V-block pushed into a dummy belt rim) had failed completely by the time he reached Quarter Bridge, and his sidecar brake failed a few minutes later when the nipple pulled off the operating cable.

Harry Langman, although he crashed out, had still managed to set the fastest lap of the race on his Scott outfit. The *Isle of Man Times* was very supportive of the new event, stating that:

> An exceedingly large number of thrills must have been afforded to the crowds round the Course by the spectacular performance of both riders and sidecar passengers. It was a race to test the will of the driver, the courage of the passenger, and the quality of the machine. The experiment of initiating a Sidecar Race for the improvement of that today rather unwieldy machine was a good one, worthy of encouragement. It is only by experience gained in such a thorough test as a road race that the faults of this article can be remedied and made safer for the general public to use.[4]

In 1924 sidecar racing was less of a novelty – people had become used to the sight of acrobatic passengers, juddering brakes and squealing tyres. Among the passengers this year was a young

Manx rider, Arthur Kinrade. His driver, Ernie Longman, had arrived on the Isle of Man with no one to act as his 'ballast', so he toured the motor workshops of Douglas, looking for a willing young mechanic to partner him, and at Callister's Garage on St George's Street in the town he had found 18-year-old apprentice Kinrade, who offered his services. Success eluded them, and they were forced to retire, but better results would come for Kinrade in the following year. Now though Freddie Dixon set the pace for half the race distance before his engine blew up. George Grinton, on the faster of the 588 Nortons, with an improved four-speed gearbox, had the nipple pull off his throttle cable on the on the first lap and rode the rest of the race pulling the cable by hand to finish fifth and last. This gave Tucker an easy victory at a slower speed than he had managed the previous year when he only managed third place.

In 1925 there was a better entry of eighteen starters, and the race distance was increased from three laps to four. In consequence, most of the passengers had to make room for long-range tanks carrying extra petrol, or in some cases alcohol fuel. The event offered the promise of a repeat of the Langman–Dixon duel of 1923, with both men setting records in practice. In the race, however, it did not materialise, as Langman's two-speed transmission failed on the first lap, and Freddie Dixon again blew up his engine at half distance. Len Parker on the second-string Douglas stepped into the breach left by Dixon to challenge the Nortons of Grinton, Taylor and Tucker. The loudest cheers from the crowd were for Grinton, who this year had recruited Manx passenger Arthur Kinrade. On the third lap, the *Isle of Man Examiner*, giving a blow by blow account offered the rather puzzling statement:

> The Ramsey marshal reports that Tinkler has gone through 'like blue h___' [hell] with his passenger trailing on the ground. This report is qualified with an observation that these men are brothers – both vegetarians, teetotallers, and non-smokers.[5]

Tucker's engine also later failed, Taylor was slowed by a throttle cable that repeatedly came out of the twist grip, and Grinton, who could probably have won, misunderstood a pit signal. He thought it meant he was winning by three minutes whereas in fact it was three seconds, and the race went to Parker. Grinton and Kinrade nevertheless managed third place, earning them bronze replicas.

The most intriguing machine to complete the race was perhaps the 500cc Dunelt, which finished sixth, ridden by Owen Bridcutt. This machine was so unusual as to be almost experimental. Produced by Dunelt & Elliotts of Birmingham, it had two magnetos firing plugs in different parts of the detachable alloy head, which was held down by three through bolts to the crankcase. Big ports and a big carburettor fed large quantities of alcohol fuel to the big single two-stroke with its double-diameter piston, with much of the fuel being used for internal cooling and going straight out of the exhaust. The sidecar race was the only event in which the Dunelt could compete, because of the vast quantities of alcohol fuel that it consumed in order to keep cool. Enough could not have been carried on a solo.

Yet in spite of the spectacle that they provided, the sidecar races at the TT were initially short-lived – the class was dropped after 1925 after pressure from manufacturers, who believed that racing the outfits around the Isle of Man was not helping their image as a reliable and safe form of family transport! The Auto-Cycle Union (ACU) issued a statement that read:

> The Sidecar Race has hitherto tended to develop a type of sidecar outfit of very little use for touring and the type of publicity which this particular race has attracted is liable to give the general public a wrong idea of the character of sidecar outfits and to obscure their great advantages for safe and comfortable travelling.
>
> While the Committee was aware that the engines of sidecar outfits underwent a severer test than those of solo machines, it is thought that similar results could be achieved in a fairer manner by extending the distance of the solo races. A further advantage which will accrue from the reduction in the number of races is the largely increased value which will result from a win in any of the three races retained.[6]

With this kind of attitude, it can only be considered fortunate that the application of a one-armed stunt rider, Eric Peacock, to participate in the 1925 sidecar TT was refused by the authorities! Certainly, at least one of the competitors thought the sidecar TT contributed more to the development of the motorcycle than did the solo races. George Tucker wrote in December 1925:

> Why do so many retirements come about in long distance sidecar races as compared with similar solo events? In my opinion it is certainly because of the greater stresses on the motorcycle generally. Four laps of the sidecar TT are also, in my opinion, a greater test of the machine than seven laps solo, although that becomes automatically a greater test of the man. I sincerely think that the sidecar TT race would bring us a better machine more quickly than a solo one. If thoughtfully organised it would even be better for the manufacturers from an advertising point of view than it has been in the past.[7]

Though no written evidence of it has so far been found, more than one veteran of the 1920s sidecar TT races later claimed that an ACU regulation insisted that the passenger must keep his feet in the sidecar at all times. This assertion is borne out by study of the numerous photographs of outfits in action during those three years. No matter what acrobatic pose is being adopted by the passenger, his feet are always in the chair. Contrast this with photos of speedway and grass tracking events from the 1930s, when passengers are sometimes seen standing on footrests outboard of the sidecar wheel.

If it was true that it was the antics of the passengers that were giving sidecars a bad name on the high street, then the ACU might have overcome this by simply tightening the regulation and insisting that the passenger remain seated (indeed some have suggested that this was why Dixon went to such effort to design the banking sidecar, in anticipation of such a rule change). Why they did not remains something of a mystery.

Dixon for his part went on to even greater things, and remains the only man to have won a Tourist Trophy on two, three and four wheels. In motorcar racing, he also set a lap record at Brooklands that was never beaten. His legacy on the Isle of Man lives on, in that one of the two sidecar Mercury statuettes for which drivers and passengers compete is named the Frederick Dixon Trophy.

However, the question of the sidecar TT, and the real reason that it was abandoned, continued to rumble on into the late 1920s. In 1927 J.R. Strong, motoring correspondent of the *Leeds Mercury*, opined:

> The possibility of the sidecar race being revived [has] not [been] forgotten. The question was considered by the Competitions Committee in consultation with the Motorcycle Manufacturers' Union, who agreed that no passenger machine race should be held, as the same reasons which caused its abandonment in 1926 were still valid.
>
> At the same time it is difficult to believe that the sidecar machine is so fast or reliable, or has passed its sphere of usefulness, to an extent which justifies its exclusion from TT races. The principal objection – that passengers in a sidecar race are, in the opinion of the public, in great danger – can easily be removed. Why not reinstate the race with a 'dead load' instead of a live load in the sidecars?[8]

In 1933 the ACU made an abortive attempt to restart the sidecar TT, announcing it in the race schedule that year and then cancelling it only twenty-nine days before it was due to run, on the grounds that not enough entries had been received. Only ten applications had been made, and it seems that of the ten only two came from manufacturers (these being Excelsior and Vincent HRD), the rest being privateers. The ACU received a good deal of criticism for its decision, and the fact that it had given no advanced warning that the plug would be pulled if more entries were not received. It was also pointed out that the ACU had previously run a race (the 1925 Ultra Lightweight) with only seven entries. Vincent HRD were particularly aggrieved, having spent £250 in developing a competitive outfit – a lot of money in 1933, enough in fact to purchase a small house.

Professor Low, chairman of the ACU, claimed to be supportive of a new sidecar TT race, stating that it was high time an event with some degree of novelty was added to the TT programme. He pointed the finger at lack of interest from the big manufacturers, but who can blame them. It would have required a great deal of investment to produce a competitive machine, Norton would almost certainly have won it anyway, and things had moved on from the 1920s. By now there was little or no commercial market for the sidecar – it was no longer the form of transport to which most families aspired. The Austin 7 had largely displaced it, for the middle classes at any rate, and the van versions of the Austin had done for the milk float and other adaptations of the commercial sidecar. When sidecars did eventually return to the TT schedule, it would be purely for the glory of racing.

Chapter 2

The Return

The next attempt by the ACU to bring sidecar racing back to the Isle of Man was prompted by the success of the FIM World Championship for sidecars, which had started in 1949. It had first been suggested for inclusion at the 1953 TT meeting, using the Willaston Circuit in Douglas, which had been used for motor car racing. This, however, had initially been rejected by Tynwald, the island's parliament. The powers that be on the Isle of Man were divided over whether to give their support to four-wheeled racing, or back the ACU proposal. Some felt that car racing had had its day, others that the TT race schedule was crowded enough already. The Tynwald Race Committee, however, was swayed by arguments that a sidecar TT might become a popular attraction at a rival holiday resort in Britain, and so eventually threw their weight behind it, pledging financial support to cover the increased cost of policing and other overheads. As late as November 1953 discussions were still ensuing over which course would be used. The Clypse Course (previously used for bicycle racing) was one proposal, others included the aforementioned Willaston Circuit, and even a new course that went down Broadway, left along the Douglas Promenade to King Edward Road and went back to the Grandstand via Onchan.

In the meantime, the ACU had been working to overcome lingering opposition from within the motorcycle industry, and this melted away once it became clear that it was mooted that sidecars should run on the Isle of Man's shorter Clypse Course, which would also accommodate the 125cc solo race. This circuit started from the TT Grandstand, but turned right at Parkfield Corner instead of continuing down Bray Hill, and headed out towards the Clypse Reservoir from which it took its name. Riders returned via Onchan, turning right at the Manx Arms, then left at Signpost corner to return to the Grandstand via Governor's Dip.

Stan Dibben had been a Norton test rider when he was asked to assist factory sidecar ace Eric Oliver who, as he put it, 'needed some ballast' to help him get an idea of how spring frames would work. The two struck up a friendship and Oliver asked him to become his passenger full time. Together the duo won the 1953 sidecar World Championship. Stan recalled:

> Eric had had a very tough war, he was a Flight Engineer on Lancaster bombers and he did more than two tours of operation at a time when Lancaster bombers were lucky to complete one tour ... He was tough, he was a very shrewd man, a good businessman. If he said he'd pay you a quid he paid you a quid, not a penny less or penny more. He was very good. We had long discussions about how to ride a sidecar, because I realised there was a bit more to it than just being a passenger. I had long discussions with Eric in terms of weight, leverage and windage ratios. We had

to get that lot right. Eric was very good at demonstrating what he wanted by his size 12 foot in the middle of my back, going at somewhere like 100 miles an hour, which is good fun! But he certainly taught me how to ride a sidecar, he was very good.

[The outfit] was [powered by] an ordinary 500 Norton Manx racing machine. Absolutely standard, with slightly different gear ratios obviously. But they were perfectly standard gearboxes, everything about it was standard, with an ordinary front exit sidecar ... The hand holds have to be very precisely placed on the thing, so that you can move around.

In January 1954 I came over [to the Island] with Eric Oliver and [1952 World Champion] Cyril Smith to proof ride the Clypse Course, which we did. And it was then of course that sidecars came back into the Isle of Man ... The roads were closed from the start, up to Creg ny Baa and then down through Onchan for us – it was very interesting actually. It was to check the circuit itself, get our opinion of the circuit, to get some idea of lap times as well, which was very important of course.[1]

That inaugural sidecar TT on the Clypse Course in 1954 was a memorable one for another reason – it was the first appearance of the glamorous Inge Stoll, who passengered Frenchman Jacques Drion. She was widely admired for her skill at the time, but there was a foretaste of the controversy that greeted the arrival of Beryl Swain in the solo races some years later when the Motorcycle Manufacturers Association wrote to the Tynwald

Race Committee to protest about a woman participant. These objections were brushed aside, and to those who continued to object the *TT Special* pointed out that she was perfectly within her rights to compete, for while ACU rules stated that a sidecar driver had to be a male over the age of 18, for a passenger it was merely enough for them to be over 18. That she should be so good was not surprising when one considered her background. Her father was one of the finest sidecar drivers in Germany in pre-war days, so Inge was born into an atmosphere of 'chair-racing'. He was her first driver, immediately after the Second World War and taught her all the 'tricks of the trade'; Inge proved to be an adept pupil, and she and Drion finished with a creditable fifth place. The duo returned to the TT three years later, but were both sadly killed thereafter while racing in Czechoslovakia.

The race proved to be as thrilling as expected. The main challenger to the Oliver-Smith monopoly was Peter 'Pip' Harris. Without a major factory supporting him, Harris mainly confined himself to domestic events, but he felt that even this was less than a level playing field, and that Oliver exerted undue influence on Norton to prevent them from providing other British riders with the latest equipment. Harris remembered:

> It's generally thought that he had been invited to drive for Gilera and that he used that offer to blackmail Norton into giving less help to the rest of the domestic competition. I could beat all the other drivers, and I might well have beaten Oliver, except that his bike was always about 10mph better on top speed than anyone else's.[2]

As evidence, Harris cited the fact that when he finally persuaded Norton to sell him a twin-cam top end for his engine (at full retail price with no discount) it turned out to produce less power than his original single-cam version at only 5,000rpm. The charitable way to look at it was not that it had been deliberately tampered with, but was just not set up correctly, so Harris and his father took it back to Nortons. Irascible race manager Joe Craig told them that all of the race technicians were too busy to look at it, but the pair slipped into the workshop anyway and found a mechanic who clearly hadn't read the memo and put it right in about half an hour!

As the flag was dropped on that first post-war sidecar TT, Harris shot forward from the second rank of the grid, but Oliver took the lead with Les Nutt in the chair. He was closely pursued by Cyril Smith, now passengered by Dibben, who recalled:

> I can remember if there was gravel on the road and we had people a bit close up behind that we wanted to get rid of I'd rub my shoulder in the road and shower them with gravel – if it was the Germans behind us I'd give them a shower of stones to get rid of them! That worked very well! But there was no ill feeling there, it was all part of the business … It was all in a jocular vein, we weren't too serious about it.[3]

Meanwhile, Fritz Hillebrand battled Harris for third place. As the race progressed, Smith and Dibben retired with engine trouble, promoting Hillebrand to third. He would eventually finish second with Harris also a retirement after his brakes failed – as he tried to out brake Hillebrand's hydraulic BMW anchors – and he ploughed into a bank at Morney Three pitching his passenger Graham Holder over the top of the sidecar. Another British rider, Bill Boddice, would finish a creditable sixth, despite having overturned his outfit and having to pit in order to check for structural damage. Boddice, an electrical engineer from Smethwick in Staffordshire, was a familiar figure on British short circuits, having started his career just after the war on grass track races in the Midlands. In 1952 he had been awarded the Watsonian Trophy for best overall performance in the year.

However, the World Championship in 1954 would not belong to Norton, but to BMW, and this would set the pattern for the next twenty years. Perhaps the most successful engine in sidecar TT history, BMW's legendary RS54 (RS standing for *Rennsport* or racing sport in English) was first introduced to the public at the 1953 Frankfurt International Bicycle and Motorcycle Exhibition. This bevel-shaft, flat twin 'boxer' engine was built solely for racing. It does not have a generator and was not a derivative of a production motor. Neither has it ever found its way into series production. The bevel shaft layout of the engine was known in German as a *Koenigswelle* or king shaft, because the circular, toothed bevel gear atop a vertical shaft was reminiscent of a king wearing a crown. BMW had reasoned that the best way to win national and international championships was by creating a pool of good international private and semi-works riders, all mounted on distinctive and recognisable BMW machines. Thus they developed a production road racing machine in which to mount their engine, which was to be available in both solo and sidecar versions. The sidecar machines featured different frames, front forks and brakes, and 19in wheels were supplied as standard. The rider's seat was short and flat, and bolted to the motorcycle was the works sidecar, manufactured by the firm of Royal, in Munich.

In fact, the sale price of these machines did not cover the manufacturing cost, but the company felt that the resulting financial loss would be more than offset by the publicity and prestige that would result from a World Championship win. However, their resources were not limitless, and one way of containing and minimising this loss was to restrict the availability of the machines. This limited availability also had the effect of encouraging the desirability of the motorcycles and led to something of a myth or cult status growing up around the RS54. At the same time as introducing the new engine, the factory team was reduced to a single solo rider and Wilhelm Noll/Fritz Cron at sidecar events. The following year the team was officially disbanded, and from then on the racing sport department under Max Klankermeier supplied and maintained engines for a stable of riders including Max Deubel, Florian Camathias, Fritz Scheidegger, Georg Auerbacher, Siegfried Schauzu, Johann Attenberger, and finally Heinz Luthringshauser. They offered varying degrees of support, with some riders receiving more than others. Frenchman Jacques Drion received a factory engine, as did Swiss rider Camathias, but the majority who did so were German. British riders Pip Harris and Colin Seeley were purely privateers with no factory support, despite using BMW machinery at times.

BMW also controlled the competition among the top-level RS riders by limiting who was supplied immediately with the latest improved parts, and making others wait. Later there was also a restrictive spare parts policy of 'new for old'. This had the intention both of preventing the creation of engines assembled from worn-out parts, and discouraging the use of non-BMW manufactured parts, which it was thought by the company would contribute to the improved reliability of their engines on the race track. In fact, it had the opposite effect in many instances. New parts were often needed at short notice, on the race track itself when these components were many miles away in Munich, and often on a Sunday when the factory was closed anyway. It also had the undesired effect of encouraging the production of a black market in unauthorised inferior copies of BMW parts, which resulted in engine failures that actually damaged the firm's reputation for reliability.

Back on the Isle of Man, the 1955 sidecar TT offered thrills galore, and it was regarded by many as Britain's last chance of securing a trophy on the Island that year, as all of the other races had gone to 'foreign' machines. Eric Oliver gallantly battled the BMWs of Walter Schneider and Wilhelm Noll until he was forced to retire when passenger Eric Bliss sustained an eye injury, resulting from smashed goggles from a stone thrown up at Ballanard Road. From Ballacoar Corner came the report that Willy Faust (in his only TT appearance) had collided with Derek Yorke (Norton). The BMW outfit was sent somersaulting through the air, but both Faust and his passenger Karl Remmert escaped unhurt. They quickly righted their combination and continued with a buckled sidecar wheel. Yorke and his passenger (R.G. Eden) also escaped injury. So far ahead were the BMWs that Faust was able to continue in third place, despite the delay. He retired at the end of the lap. The crash of Wilhem Noll and Fritz Cron when in the lead was spectacular and frightening for those who witnessed it. Fortunately it resulted in neither driver nor passenger suffering more than shock. Noll had got past Ballacoar according to an eyewitness, but on the succeeding bend did not appear to straighten up the machine after taking the corner. The outfit, with the two men, was thrown into the air. The model righted itself and the men in coming down curled themselves up in order to make as soft a landing as possible. They landed on the tarmac, then sprang to their feet and got out of the way. The BMW with its sidecar travelled down the road for another 100 yards and was quickly removed by the marshals. Schneider took the victory.

Somewhat disenchanted with not receiving much assistance from Norton, even after Oliver had effectively retired, Pip Harris must have been encouraged in 1955 when he was finally offered a little works support from Matchless. Oddly, it came via the trade rather than the manufacturer, and at the Bemsee (BMRC) Annual Dinner it was the Mobil representative who asked him if he would like a works G45. Naturally, he said yes, and bizarrely found that while the engine was free, he had to pay for the gearbox! Rated at 60bhp, the G45 gave 5 or 6 more horsepower than the Norton, but although he used it for four months, and finished third in the 1955 TT, Pip was never very happy with its characteristics.

Stan Dibben and Cyril Smith's TT outing in 1955 was memorable for all the wrong reasons, however, after an incident at Edge's Corner, recalled by Stan:

> I can remember on this occasion out towards Cronk ny Mona a farmer had dug a hole in a hedge to put a gateway in, and the kerb wasn't absolutely parallel to the road, and there was a lump of stuff sticking out, and we hit that lump of stuff and I had fifteen stitches through my nose, so we didn't finish that race. [Cyril] stopped and they took me off to Nobles, I had one night in Nobles and I was back up at the pits the following day.
>
> [The machines] were exactly the same as Eric's, perfectly standard 500 Manx Nortons, only the gear ratios had to be modified. When we got onto Featherbed frames we had to alter the steering geometry because the standard geometry on a Manx for solo work, the trail is much longer for solo work than it is for sidecars, so we had to shorten the trail. We used different front forks with a different attachment for the front wheel spindle, it had a big boss on the front.[4]

Although Cyril toured on without ballast, just beyond Creg ny Baa he turned the outfit over and suffered a broken arm, and so very quickly joined his passenger in hospital.

The following year saw the only Isle of Man appearance of Australian sidecar star Bob Mitchell, who having dominated three-wheeled racing down under was trying to make his name in Europe. With Eric Bliss in the chair, Bob had hoped to qualify for a grant from the Auto Cycle Council of Australia to help with expenses at the TT, but their representative in the UK, Australian former Sunbeam works rider and GP winner Arthur 'Digger' Simcock, refused to nominate him, saying he was not up to the standard required! Eric Oliver helped out by paying their entry fee, but otherwise rewards were slight at what was supposed to be the world's premier motorcycling event. Although the ACU of Great Britain put up substantial sums to attract the European teams, British-based privateers like Mitchell were often given the cold shoulder. Despite the slur, Mitchell and Bliss took confidently to the sometimes treacherous Clypse circuit, and held third place in the race until the clutch refused to disengage, making the process of keeping off the stone walls even trickier. As he battled on, Bob waved Bill Boddice past, then wondered why he had, because he had no trouble staying with him. Still, fourth place was a fine result, particularly after his treatment by the ACCA. It was not, however, enough to bring him factory support, and at the end of the season Mitchell crated up his Norton-Watsonian outfit and headed home. The experience he had gained in Europe would lead to his complete domination of the Australian racing scene in the coming years.

From about 1956, the BMW factory ceased the supply of sidecars and frames, and thereafter limited its involvement in racing to engines and other components. Initially the motorcycle and sidecar had been separate entities, but very quickly they evolved into a single unit, which would culminate in a monocoque construction. The flat layout of the boxer engine created problems in solo racing because of its width; there was a tendency for the protruding cylinders to catch on kerbs and obstructions when cornering. Indeed Georg Auerbacher, early in his career while still a solo rider, was quoted as saying: 'The BMW flat twin is a mistaken design, it can't be ridden solo.'[5]

Yet its shallow, flat design with ample amounts of power was eminently suited for sidecar use and indeed it encouraged the lowering of the whole outfit; as early as 1956 many riders were substituting 16in wheels for the 19in ones originally supplied, in order to lower the centre of gravity. At the same time, the kneeler frame design began to become more common, with the fuel tank relocated to the sidecar and with fuel transferred across to the engine by a battery-driven pump. Most of the rider's weight was then taken by his knees. Bill Boddice was one of the few riders who for a long time resisted the growing prevalence of integral frames for both motorcycle and sidecar, stating:

> I believe in racing only genuine sidecars ... My test is this: The sidecar should be detachable so that the machine can then be wheeled away and ridden.[6]

Pip Harris now decided to return to his old Norton, and after having achieved second place in the 1956 TT, he asked Managing Director Gilbert Smith for a short-stroke works engine to use in it. In a final display of industrial intransigence – all the more inexplicable now their biggest sidecar star Eric Oliver had departed the scene – Smith claimed this was impossible. Luckily, a major Yorkshire dealer overheard the conversation and interrupted with words to the effect of: 'If you can't find an engine for Harris, you needn't bother finding the 50 Nortons

I've got on order.' Strangely enough, the short-stroke motor was delivered almost immediately! Unfortunately, the long wait did not produce the desired effect, as the motor was not to prove particularly reliable. In fact, as time marched on it effectively meant that the Manx had had its day as a sidecar machine. As a solo the frame's capabilities could still make up for a shortfall in power, but that advantage was naturally lost when the third wheel was added, and the tall motor did not lend itself to the lower and more streamlined outfits that were now emerging.

The 1957 sidecar TT was a BMW 1-2-3 with Fritz Hillebrand, Walter Schneider and Florian Camathias taking the honours on the podium. Hillebrand, the Sidecar class record holder, broke it again by a margin of one second. He produced a lap of eight minutes fifty-nine seconds, which equated to a speed of 72.07mph, on his immaculate BMW combination. The German driver, hailed as 'excellent' in the Manx newspapers, had ridden consistently throughout the 'chair' practices, as had countryman Schneider (also BMW mounted), who was second on the leader board. The driver of one sidecar machine, Graham Humby, of South Africa, was taken to hospital for observation as the result of an accident just past the Five-and-a-Half corner. There was another accident in this race, at Brandish, after which T. Leek, passenger in Charlie Freeman's Norton, was also taken to hospital for observation and with suspected leg injuries. The machine went into the corner too fast and lost wheel grip, with the result that the 'chair' became airborne and Leek was thrown on to the road. The driver was unharmed, and the two sidecar men in hospital were reported to be 'comfortable' the following morning. The return of Jaques Drion and Inge Stoll added much interest to the race, but their Norton, like that of Cyril Smith, broke down around the halfway mark. Some humour was injected into the proceedings by a small notice reading 'Nicht hinauslehnen' on the side of one 'chair' in the Sidecar event. The passenger explained that it was an inscription frequently seen on German railway carriages, and he thought it applied particularly to a sidecar passenger – the translation being 'Do not lean out'. More humour came from Fritz Hillebrand's passenger Manfred Grunwald, the man who received the loudest acclaim from the crowd at the prize presentation at the Villa Marina shortly afterwards. This was not because of his daring and brilliant work on board Hillebrand's outfit, but because of his speech to the admiring assembly:

> Thank you all on the Island, for all the help given to us by the various industries. But there is one thing we do not like – you close your pubs on Sunday and we could not get a drink.[7]

At this unexpected remark, the applause and cheers from the vast audience indicated Grunwald and Hillebrand had their sympathisers.

Stan Dibben could justifiably also claim a place in the history of sidecar racing on the Mountain circuit, for in 1957 he was back with Eric Oliver to open the roads following the Senior race that year. This was to give event organisers some idea of lap times for the anticipated return of sidecars to the 37¾-mile course. The days were numbered for the Clypse Course, with British ace Bill Boddice writing to *Motor Cycling*:

> Might I ... make an appeal to the ACU to forget the Clypse Course next year and let everyone have a proper race. This is the only thing that will ensure our entry for next year.[8]

In 1958, another female passenger made her debut on the Isle of Man – Mrs Pat Wise. The whole event had the air of a publicity stunt and was the brainchild of Eric Oliver and Ron Watson of Watsonian sidecars. In order to demonstrate the comfort and stability of a Watsonian Monaco sidecar, Oliver would ride a Norton 88 Dominator in Daytona trim (9-1 pistons, twin carbs and meggas) with the sidecar attached and a lady passenger who would sit serenely instead of performing the usual acrobatics. Pat's husband Les was a long-time friend of Eric's, and suggested his wife for the role of passenger. Their objective in the race was merely to secure a bronze replica but even this looked doubtful. In Practice Week the machine was beset with gremlins that Oliver and Les Wise struggled to overcome. This, coupled with press criticism suggesting that it was a frivolous effort, dampened Eric's mood, but he made up for technical deficiencies by meticulous attention to the course; his skill in cornering also more than made up for a lack of speed on the straights. Afterwards, Mrs Wise recounted the exhilaration of the race itself:

> Down went the flag – we were off! My most vivid memory of the start was of the outfit storming through a gap that

appeared momentarily between one of the competitors and the scoreboard – a gap that I swear left us only a few thou' each side. Into Parkfield. Not last by any means, then Willaston Corner, and on down to Hillberry.

This was quite hectic, taken in one long drift, for the heat had transformed the surface into a sea of wet tar. Eric was superb here, and the conditions didn't seem to affect our speed at all. On to Brandish and the Creg, which seemed painfully slow – revs kept down to 6-4. Round the Creg we were one of the fastest, and suddenly, lo and behold, I saw three outfits on the grass verge. ('Don't suppose it could be Schneider, but anyway it has delayed three of those in front of us!')

Eric was terrific over the four miles to Hall's Corner, and for me it was the most thrilling section of all. Whitebridge, with the grip rolled back to keep revs to a reasonable limit, and so on to the Manx Arms, not braking until after the Memorial. When the stoppers did come on, I felt that 1 was going straight through the screen! It was a bit of an effort for the 'old girl' at the Nursery Bends, in spite of spectacular drifting and, at times, with one wheel off the deck. Next one up was Signpost, and then we joined the Mountain Course, Governor's Bridge, and up the Glencrutchery Road to the start. Slight panic here, as I couldn't see Les in the pit. (Must make sure of his position next time round.)

Parkfield again and up to the Creg. Someone passed us and there was nothing we could do about it. We got on his tail through the Five Mile and tried to pass – no room.

After Hall's Corner, he pulled away from us. I discovered that poor Bill Beevers was one of those out on the first lap (not at the Manx Arms, but near the Creg) and he laughingly held out a cup of tea as we flew past!

We continued to circulate, and then sighs of relief, there at the pits was Les; we gave the thumbs up! By this time the tar at Hillberry was really bad, but it didn't bother Eric. We had a friend giving us signals at the Five Mile. Things were going fine, with the motor maintaining its healthy roar, as we maintained our schedule.

Going up to Brandish on the fifth lap, Schneider was on our tail, and he passed just before the corner. We were still with him on the way out. but then he just rocketed away. Next to pass was Camathias, and then Ritter. On the sixth lap, we got the signal that a fill-up would be necessary – so Schneider could not lap us twice! We kept going, very lonely now, with not another outfit in sight.

Towards the end of the eighth lap we prepared to come in. Eric slackened the filler cap and I felt that I would like to help, but there was nothing that I could do. The engine cut out and Les gave Eric the hose – 1-2-3-4-5 seconds. The hose was literally thrown back at Les, and petrol from it splashed into my face; Eric pushed the outfit off – all eight hundred pounds of it! About six paces, the now familiar roar – and we were off, back in the fray again for the last lap.

The crowds gave us a great reception on this lap, cheering, shouting and waving programmes at us. Round the Manx Arms for the last time, now Governor's

Bridge and the Clock Tower. The chequered flag – we had made it!⁹

Passenger John Chisnall was the regular partner of Sheffield motorcycle dealer Bill Beevers in these years. The duo raced at all of the European Grands Prix in this era, as part of what was known as the Continental Circus, but also found time to compete in the major British events. For him, the TT was the 'Queen of Races'. He remembered his first experience on the Isle of Man when he passengered for Charlie Freeman:

> We eventually arrived at the magic Island where the atmosphere was and still is 100% motorbikes. The snarl of the engines being warmed up, the smell of Castrol-R pervading the neighbourhood of the paddock, the enthusiasm of the locals who, it must be remembered, were severely restricted in their movements; those roads forming part of the course were closed every morning and evening for practice and for most of the time on race days … It seemed that every Manxman (and woman) was a keen fan of the races and moreover, as knowledgeable about the event and its history as any motorcycle racing buff.[10]

He was equally impressed by the accommodation that awaited them:

> We riders were treated as stars, whether it was by the white-helmeted bobbies turning a blind eye to racing bikes being warmed up or waving them through Douglas's

public streets on their way to the paddock, or the pride felt by landladies who had one or more competitors staying in their B & B ... Once having established good digs [we] would return to the same landlady year after year ... I always stayed with Mrs Hunter in Murrays Road, as did [sidecar driver] Brian Green and next door was Cyril Smith. This sort of thing gave the TT a comfortable feeling, something to rely on.

And these landladies treated one like VIPs, arranging meals around the practice or race times so as not to inconvenience us. Our morning practice at 6am meant they had to be up with a warming cuppa and then holding back breakfast until after you'd finished.[11]

The landlady looked after him 'like a mother' and so grateful was he that he left the silver replica that he won that year with her as a thank you. For her part the landlady was pleased because other riders had promised something similar but none had actually kept their word. Chisnall's next competitive TT appearance was in 1958 with Beevers and his Manx Norton. He remembered:

We hit trouble on lap one when the clutch nut came loose just before we reached the corners known as The Edges. We kept going but gear-change was difficult and we lost a lot of speed, being overtaken by several pairs ... When we arrived at the Morney–Begoade section, a series of left/right bends with high banks either side just before Hall Corner, there was grass and earth all over the road and my first fears were for Eric and Pat but it was in fact Charlie Freeman. We stopped where he had clipped the bank to see if we could help but apart from a broken finger with the bone poking through his glove, Charlie was uninjured, though not so shaken that he couldn't find the breath to blame his passenger Terry Harrison – but I knew Charlie and his risk-taking of old and took this with a pinch of salt.[12]

By now, Beevers was tiring of the unreliability of the Norton, which dropped valves with annoying regularity, and had heard via Florian Camathias that there was an ex-works BMW engine available at a car dealership in Bad Driburg in West Germany. He and Chisnall headed straight from the Nürburgring, where they had been competing, to the dealership and found out that the story was true. The engine was mounted in a racing outfit, and after some negotiation and horse trading Beevers secured the machine. All that remained was for Chisnall to remove the right-hand-mounted sidecar and add one on the left-hand side.

In Europe, all of the most successful drivers had now switched to BMW engines, and the boxer twins were sweeping all before them, being powerful, reliable, and with a layout ideal for the genre. In 1959, Pip Harris also decided that if he couldn't beat them, he would have to join them, so he and fellow British driver Jack Beeton purchased a BMW race engine from Australian racer Jack Forest. Pip went over to Munich to have the motor rebuilt and to buy a new Rennsport race frame for it. He remembered:

They did everything while I was there, and were incredibly efficient. They were also extremely expensive, charging an astronomical £1500 in a bill that even included the petrol they'd used to wash the parts![13]

The next time that they were in West Germany, Chisnall and Beevers also took their Rennsport unit back to BMW to be serviced, and were equally impressed by the efficiency of the mechanics, whose attention to detail included checking a crankshaft for wear using a micrometre on a stand, instead of holding it in the hand, as human body heat might cause an infinitesimally small degree of error in the reading!

Harris and Beeton had split the initial cost of their outfit, but it quickly became obvious that sharing a machine was not going to work. Fortunately, Beeton had reached the age at which he was ready to retire, so Pip bought out his share and became the sole user.

The BMW-supplied Rennsport frame was intended for solo racing, and like the Norton Featherbed it proved less than ideal when allied to a Watsonian chair in the sidecar class. Now the trend – started by Eric Oliver – was towards ever lower and more integrated outfits. Not one to claim any great mechanical or developmental skills, Pip again decided that he had to follow the prevailing fashion.

I basically set the engine, and myself, between the wheels, and asked my brother John to join everything together.[14]

The result, welded up from Reynold's 531 tubing and developed over the next few seasons, was incredibly successful. Pip did not have any difficulty in converting to a kneeler chassis, after years in the saddle:

> On the contrary, it seemed very easy, I felt part of the machine, and it seemed really natural to drift it round corners.[15]

The performance of Harris's BMW outfit, and of passenger Ray Campbell, can be judged by the way it led the 1959 sidecar TT for several laps until the drive shaft broke, forcing a retirement. Despite always being one step behind the Continental riders when it came to machinery, Harris remained full of praise for the BMW engines and their makers.

> I lost touch with the factory when my initial contact, Muller, had a heart attack and retired but it didn't really matter because the long-stroke engine was incredibly reliable.[16]

Nevertheless, victory in the 1959 race, the last to be run on the Clypse Course, went to Walter Schneider and Hans Strauss. Six of the top seven finishers in this race were BMW mounted, and as a new decade opened, the firm's near stranglehold on sidecar racing would only occasionally be challenged.

Chapter 3

German Domination

By now, the writing was on the wall for the unpopular Clypse Course. It was not well suited for spectators, with the sections out by the Clypse Reservoir after which it was named being particularly hard to access. Above all, it was too short and it was becoming harder for the TT organisers to accommodate the growing number of competitors in the sidecar event. However, when the sidecar TT did eventually return to the Mountain Course in 1960 there were doubts initially over whether three-wheelers would survive three laps of the Mountain climb, as well as a race distance nearly twice that of any other World Championship event. Yet of the thirty starters that year, twenty crews would make it to the finish line, proving the doubters wrong.

Eric Oliver was reunited with Stan Dibben for the TT in 1960; for Stan it was the first time riding in anger on the big course since competing in the 1954 Senior race, but it was all to come undone in spectacular fashion during Wednesday morning practice, as Stan remembered:

> Eric got on to me one day ... He just phoned me one day and said, 'I want to do the TT, do you want to do it with me?' Simple as that! So of course I said, 'Yeah, fine it'll be great'. By this time I was in the industry, in

the chain industry, and I was coming over anyway, giving trade support … So it was perfectly normal for me to say I'd do it. [But] the topography had changed, trees had grown, people had changed the colour of their fences and gateposts which was not very kind!

We'd walked through a lot of the more difficult corners like the bottom of Begarrow, for example, Eric said I can go through here flat out if I can use all of the road, so I said, 'You use all of the road, and I'll look after the sidecar!' Our standing start lap was seven miles an hour quicker than anyone else, and the flying lap was going wonderfully well, and then on the left hander above Guthries the front forks broke off, and Eric got propelled over the fence, down the mountainside, and I got caught up in a wire fence. They had to get a pair of pliers to cut the wire that was around my neck.

The front forks were Earls-type forks, that were bolted on through the headstock, and the bottom bolt had been over-tightened, and the bottom bolt let go, and then the front end was held on with one bolt which wasn't strong enough to do it. The whole lot, the front forks, the fairing and the front wheel went off up the road on their own. I was alright, I was only in hospital one night, then I was back up the pits again doing my usual work. But it more or less finished Eric.[1]

The BMW entry was particularly strong once again, with the first appearance of Max Deubel on the Isle of Man. Deubel was to become one of the best known of the BMW riders, not least because he chose to distinguish his machine from the other outfits (which mostly also had white fairings) by use of a distinctive cartoon on the nose, showing two mischievous boys, Max and Moritz. They were created by the author–illustrator Wilhelm Busch in 1865. The boys were popularly renowned in Germany as being quite a nuisance to other people, so perhaps this was also part of the reason they were chosen. Deubel remembered his initial hesitation when confronted with the circuit:

> Of course, my experiences and stories with the Isle of Man began with my passenger of those years, Horst Hoehler, when in 1960 we travelled with the night boat and arrived at dawn. Only a few hours later we had the first training session. After the end of the first round, my thought was that you just can't learn the course and I was very worried about what would come out of it, what kind of successes might be possible.[2]

Another incident in practice for the 1960 TT served to illustrate the difference in approach between the BMW factory and the Norton equivalent. It came when Pip Harris's engine seized. Geoff Duke (at that point also riding a BMW solo machine) contacted the German factory on his behalf, and they flew a crank, barrel and pistons out to the Isle of Man in time for him to take part in the race. Not only that, but BMW rider and engineer Helmut Fath also rebuilt his engine free of charge, after which he and Pip somewhat appropriately had a duel in the race itself.

The 1960 sidecar race had further tension in store, when the German driver seized victory from his Swiss rival Florian

Camathias to take the win in dramatic style. Within sight of the finish line Fath ran out of fuel, as petrol flowed back from one tank into the other. Efforts at hand-pumping petrol into the engine failed, so his quick-thinking passenger Alfred Wohlgemuth seized the breather pipe, blew into it and forced petrol back into the empty tank, enabling them to coast across the finish line. In doing so, to the delight of TT trivia fans down the decades, Fath and Wohlgemuth broke the class lap record by the widest margin ever recorded – 28.61mph – as they chopped thirteen minutes and thirteen seconds off Freddie Dixon's record from 1925!

Rising star Max Deubel came into his own in 1961, scoring a victory at only his second appearance on the Isle of Man and setting a new lap record into the bargain. He recalled:

> Unfortunately, my passenger Horst Hoehler left at the end of the 1960 season because he wanted to continue his education, and his professional development had priority over racing. That was the reason to look for a new passenger and I think I made a very good choice with Emil Hoerner, who was with me for the last 6 years and we have had many successes together … But the [sheer] commitment that we put in personally, every free hour that we were on the island, getting to know the track on a motorbike or in a car. This then paid off for the first time in 1961 when we won the TT.[3]

For Deubel, the 1961 TT was also memorable for the fact that he had formed a close association with Mike Hailwood, who was already becoming a force to reckon with in the solo classes, and his father Stan. That year, Stan Hailwood had arranged for a telephone system all the way around the course to keep him informed of Mike's progress (and that of his competitors). He invited Deubel to help him to test it and also make use of it.

The 1961 sidecar TT was not without tragedy, however, when on the second lap Swiss passenger Marie Lambert, aged 26, was killed when the BMW outfit driven by her husband Claude suffered a rear-wheel seizure and skidded before overturning at the Cuttings, before Brandish Corner.

There was less success for Deubel the following year in as much as he was forced to retire in the race, but not before he had raised the lap record to over 90mph for the first time, an outstanding achievement that captured the world's attention. He continued:

> Then there is the question of 1962 and setting a record there, which was quite sensational at the time. But coming back to the effort we put in, riding, riding, riding the track ... and getting to know it and it paid off because the engine, the chassis and everything was the same as in 1961 ... Now a few words about the season and the TT race in 1962. That was a very, very tight race between Camathias-Burkhardt and us. We were in front, started 20 seconds ahead of the Camathias team. And our equipment was exactly the same as it was in 1961. But the increased speed came from an intense effort to get to know the track. All the opportunities when we had an hour to ride on a motorcycle or drive a car around the

circuit paid off. It was all done to improve our knowledge about the TT course.

In general, on the road, on the track, in the race, there was a fight for everything that was at stake. But when the flag had sunk and we were back in the paddock, there was generally great camaraderie, a willingness to help and everyone helped where they could if they had the opportunity. It was a different time and it was a different mentality than today. You have to see that very clearly. Maybe a better time too.[4]

Deubel enjoyed a high level of support from BMW's Munich headquarters, even though the engine he was using was only on loan from the factory:

Gustle Lachermair accompanied us often to the race circuits, whom I picked up in Munich together with spare parts when I first received works support for the TT race on the Isle of Man in 1961. Afterwards I chauferred [sic] him back to Munich. The support was very worthwhile during such a race event. Although the engine was generally very reliable there often was something to repair between practising and racing and the sidecar outfit had to be adjusted to the circuit and the weather conditions. I myself have never been much of a mechanic. As a trained toolmaker I was not very familiar with the engine. With only one single exception I completely relied on Lachermair. After not finishing the 1962 TT race he was more angry because of the technical failure than I was.[5]

By this point in time the only serious British threat to the dominance of BMW was to come from the BSA factory in Birmingham, Norton's challenge having by now faded (though the firm would continue to be a force in solo racing into the early 1970s). More precisely, it was the BSA A65 engine that was to become the motor of choice for many British sidecar competitors in the late 1960s and into the early 1970s. However, it must be stated that the firm itself had little involvement (or interest) in its development in a sidecar application, and this was due more to the skill and dedication of enthusiasts both outside and inside the factory. Chris Vincent, with Eric Bliss in the chair, delivered BSA's first ever sidecar win in 1962. Birmingham-born Vincent had been a factory bike tester with Norton in his early career, and his progression to road racing came via speedway. Of that memorable victory he recalled:

> Never ever anywhere could you reproduce what the crowd did for me that day. I swear that some of the crowd was the wrong side of the wall, they were my side of the wall, and towards the end of the race, I'm coming down the Mountain, and especially corners like Brandish, Creg ny Baa, Signpost, they were all incredible. That was the days of the British [motorcycle] industry, and the British [motorcycle] enthusiasts, and very large crowds of people, very enthusiastic for what I was eventually going to do [which was] a British win. It is one that I couldn't ever forget. It was a success that pleased a lot of people.[6]

It was often said that BSA race engines were confined to the 'Birmingham mafia', the small clique of riders from that area who had links to the factory and who could get access to racing engines and components, in much the same way that BMW supported a small group of German riders. The latest among these was Bavarian-born Georg Auerbacher, who was to make his TT debut at this year's event. His compatriot, racing enthusiast and photographer Karl Schleuter of Bonn was with him, and he recalled many years later:

> The first lap for Auerbacher on the TT was in 1962 with me in my BMW R60 combination. We made a stop at Ramsey and Georg said, what was this a long lap! But I had to tell him, it was only half of the races track! The first practise lap was in the evening. Fritz Scheidegger had not arrived, so his passenger Horst Burghardt made the first lap with Auerbacher. But only a short one! At Braddan Bridge, Auerbacher was going straight on, but Horst, he knew the S bend. So there was a crash! After this, there was a new point on the TT course. We called it Auerbacher Bridge.[7]

In 1963, most of the TT competitors had endured a punishing schedule, coming from a race in France at Le Touquet, then to Brands Hatch for an international meeting, followed by a road journey on to the Isle of Man. Eccentric Swiss rider Florian Camathias, having suffered a breakdown in his Citroën transporter van at Hinckley, simply unloaded his BMW-FCS outfit from the back and drove it with open exhausts all the way to Liverpool to catch the ferry – ignoring the looks of amazement on the faces of the local police as he passed through the Mersey tunnel! Among the British challengers was Matchless-mounted Colin Seeley, who recalled his arrival on the Island:

> As we left the docks we turned onto the TT circuit at Quarter Bridge heading for Union Mills and viewed the banners displayed around the circuit: 'Castrol' 'Dunlop' 'Lucas' 'Avon' 'Girling' 'BP' etc. This created a great feeling of excitement but also some apprehension. … With our Matchless G50 fitted with a six-speed Schafleitner gearbox specially for the TT I certainly thought it was possible to lap the Island at around 85mph, having averaged 82.80 [mph] for the whole race in 1962. We only needed to gain around 90 seconds per lap to achieve this speed. Our knowledge of the TT course was so much better, gaining so much experience in the last year made me confident that our goal was achievable. The six-speed box would give us an advantage over the mountain section, keeping our single cylinder on the boil. I always thought the BMW competitors benefited over the mountain climb with their extra horsepower, however from the start through the often blind corners and hedgerows to Ramsey, I thought we pretty well held our own.[8]

In 1963, riders also had to contend with a newly installed roundabout for the first time at Quarter Bridge. The racing line took them to the right of the traffic island and, to avoid confusion, signs reading 'keep left' had been covered with straw bales. This was the scene of a dramatic incident during Thursday afternoon practice when Heinz Luthringshauser and Brian Armstrong clipped the roundabout and overturned their outfit, which caught fire before throwing both men out. The straw bales were also soon alight, and although neither passenger nor rider was seriously injured they did not compete in the race. Among the other BMW riders, Max Deubel, who was normally so precise, also suffered an uncharacteristic crash at Sarah's Cottage in practice, rendering his usual passenger Emil Hoerner unfit to race. He had to quickly look around for a replacement and settled on the newcomer Barry Dungworth, in his first race on the Isle of Man.

On the day of the race there was much last-minute drama. Veteran British star Pip Harris was to start as number one, but developed a fuel leak as the warning klaxon sounded to signal the riders to assemble on the start line. Bill Boddice was first off the line, followed by Camathias, who had overhauled him by Ballacraine. Seeley remembered:

At Sulby Bridge, roughly halfway round, Fritz [Scheidegger] was ahead of Florian by 9 seconds with Kolle third and us fourth, but and the end of the first lap it was Scheidegger, Camathias, Birch, Auerbacher, Kolle with us in sixth place. Our lap time was down on 1962 by over 1mph, which was disappointing. The second lap was no better, 1.25mph down. The G50 engine just wasn't pulling as it should, fortunately the six-speed box was at least keeping us in contention.[9]

Florian Camathias, at thirty-nine years of age, with fellow countryman Alfred Herzig, went on to score their first TT win, with an average speed of 88.38mph, a new race record. He told a reporter afterwards that he had been bothered throughout the race by misfiring caused by carburettor flooding; indeed at several points in the race his engine had almost died. He took the first lap steadily, explaining:

> I had heard there was tar on the road so I was looking as I went round. I did not want to have an accident. Then I saw Scheidegger was going very quickly so I thought I would go a bit faster. But I never went very fast. It was not necessary.[10]

The almost pristine state of Camathias's rear tyre after the race testified to the fact that his win had been a comfortable one. Perhaps an even more remarkable achievement was that of the Birch brothers, fifty years before their near-namesakes the Birchalls. Allan Birch, who lost a leg in road accident in 1959, started racing just two years later in 1961. Together with his brother Peter, in the sidecar, they competed at the top level in road races all over Britain and abroad, finishing in sixth place in the 1963 sidecar World Championship. But it was at the Isle of Man TT races that the Birch brothers came to prominence riding a BMW Rennsport sidecar outfit, and from being virtually unknown they rode into third place. Allan and Peter's outfit, although good, was no match for their opponents' bikes in terms of speed, and they did not have the luxury of hydraulic brakes. Allan rode the three laps with just the front brake (which was fairly useless) at his disposal, after a piece of rag wrapped itself around the rear and put it out of action.

When searching for support, Allan and Peter had written to various suppliers of oil and tyres. Dunlop and Castrol turned them down, much to their disappointment, but Avon agreed to supply the tyres and an oil supplier in Sheffield, N.D. Nichols, agreed to provide the lubricant. When Allan and Peter went to the Avon factory they not only gave them sidecar tyres, but also put tyres on the van. They had enough tyres to last them until the TT and N.D. Nichols supplied not only oil but grease and hand cleaner, too.

When Allan then came third it gave him a great deal of satisfaction that the companies that had initially turned him down were now desperate to provide the tyres and oil. The big companies wanted to be able to advertise the fact that they had supplied to all the top three finishers, but without Allan accepting the 'gifts' they couldn't do it. Avon tyres and N.D. Nichols both published an advert stating that they had supplied to the Birch Brothers. This gave Allan just as much of a kick as his finishing place in the race. Peter even told Dunlop where they could stick their tyres, although Dunlops were dropped off nonetheless at the boarding house and at his home on Green Lane, in Poynton, Cheshire. Never one to throw things away, they stayed in his shed for many years.

Their BMW outfit was their pride and joy, but they found that it was down on power due to poor streamlining. One of their first actions on acquiring it was to add a new fairing. A fibreglass fuel tank was built into the sidecar floor, and they added hinged baffles to divide it into four compartments, in order to stop fuel surging during braking and cornering, an idea borrowed from aircraft tanks. The frame was narrowed to better accommodate Allan's knees, but they still had problems with bursting rubber shock absorbers, until Camathias put them right and on his advice they shortened and softened up the rear suspension units, and had no further trouble in that area. In fact, they had unabashed admiration for the Swiss rider, who had offered them nothing but help.

Another problem that they had overcome by the time of their dramatic TT ride was with carburettors, which at the Spanish Grand Prix earlier in the season had cost them third place through fuel starvation on left-handers. Now they had Dellortos, which they admitted had cost them a fortune, but now for the first time things were really running right. Allan added after the race:

> The Isle of Man is one of the easiest races. After the Spanish we were glad to get off the bike but we could have done another three laps of the TT course.[11]

In 1964, other British drivers had stepped up their preparations in pursuit of TT victory. Previous winner Chris Vincent was now BMW mounted, using an ultra-low outfit powered by an ex-Scheidegger long-stroke motor. The engine squatted lower and more forward than usual, necessitating a longer prop shaft to the back wheel. To get the exhausts away from under-floor fuel tanks, both pipes were on the right. The distinctive appearance of the outfit was completed by light alloy fairings. Colin Seeley, meanwhile, had acquired an ex-Camathias BMW-powered outfit, styled an FCS-B. Seeley's passenger, Wally Rawlings, was taking no chances and had added an extra chinstrap to his helmet for the TT. At the French Grand Prix a week earlier they had been black flagged when Rawlings lost his headgear, resulting in a loss of points. TT spectator John Newton remembered:

> For many sidecar fans, 1964 will be remembered as the year Camathias piloted a Gilera-4. Never before or since has an outfit sounded so wonderful! Sitting on the hedge after Braddan you could hear Camathias go down through the gears for Quarter Bridge and then up again for the straight to Braddan.[12]

The Swiss rider had been seeking an alternative to the BMW engine, and had looked at MV Agusta motors before settling on the Gilera. It had four upright inline cylinders and although it had a higher centre of gravity than the BMW engine it also had more power. Camathias also introduced larger-diameter carburettors to improve performance, but the Italian factory was not interested in supporting sidecars, and the experiment came to naught. Practice had not gone too well for the popular Swiss driver, and Deubel and Scheidegger were expected to compete for the win. Deubel led Camathias and Scheidegger from the start of the race, and when the latter retired it was down to Camathias to challenge for the laurels. However, the Gilera slowed on the final lap and Deubel scored a comfortable victory. Georg Auerbacher's BMW came in third.

In 1965 Auerbacher, now with new mechanic Josef Ried, managed third place again behind Deubel and Scheidegger. In what was a thrilling battle, a soft rear tyre forced Deubel into some alarming slides, but it did not prevent the West German ace from raising his 1962 lap record to 91.80mph on the last of his three laps. Rival Scheidegger had been fastest in practice, and led on the road, but Deubel quickly hauled him in. The challenge from Camathias soon faded when he developed clutch slip and was forced to retire. After Pip Harris did likewise with a broken gearbox, the best of the British challengers was Chris Vincent, who was beset with problems. He stopped three times on the first lap, trying to cure an air lock in a fuel pipe, then he caught his sidecar mudguard while overtaking a slower outfit and stopped again to hammer it straight. To cap it all his battery leads came adrift but amazingly he finished fifth behind Luthringshauser, the highest place of the home riders. Deubel's outfit had now delivered three wins in six races on the Isle of Man, a testament both to the preparation of the engine by Lachermair, and to the strength of his chassis (it is interesting to note that Deubel never fully adopted the 'kneeler' position, retaining an upright, seated position albeit in a much-lowered frame).

The 1966 TT took place in August due to the seamen's strike that year, and was combined with the Manx Grand Prix. For the first time a TT race – the sidecar event – was held on a Sunday, and it would prove to be one of the most controversial in the history of three-wheeled sport on the Mountain. Deubel led from the start, building a twelve-second lead, but unknown to the fans around the course, drama was beginning to unfold. Deubel's engine began to seize at Union Mills on the final lap. At almost the same time, Scheidegger had his gearbox jam at Governor's Dip as he came to the end of his second lap. So

Deubel was down on revs and Scheidegger could only change gear by crashing the box. The latter man began to eat into the former's lead, taking five seconds out of him by Ramsey, and Scheidegger snatched victory by just 0.8 seconds!

The drama was not over yet, however – a few hours later Scheidegger was disqualified when the Auto-Cycle Union was informed that he had used Esso fuel, even though he had declared it on his official entry form. Competitors were required to use Shell-BP fuel unless otherwise contracted, and Scheidegger was not contracted to Esso. The stewards backed the ACU decision and rejected his appeal, to the fury of fans and media alike, as well as fellow competitors. It took nearly three months for Scheidegger to be reinstated as winner, after the RAC (which was the ultimate arbiter in all British motor racing disputes) overturned the ACU's decision.

Auerbacher again managed third place, but remembered this as the hardest TT race of his career. The reason that he gave for this was the unwillingness of tyre manufacturers to supply softer compounds to non-works machines. Auerbacher and passenger Wolfgang Kalauch instead used hard-compound Dunlops, which proved impossible to drift. The third place that they achieved was something of a minor miracle since the duo had to coast and push all the way from Creg ny Baa. They had left the hardener out of the resin when repairing a hole in the fuel tank and ran out of petrol at Windy Corner. They struggled on as far as the Creg, before identifying the fault and settling down to push.

In 1966 there was also the debut of one of the most enduring figures in the history of the sidecar TT races, Roy Hanks. That year he was passengered by Fred Holden, whose sweet shop was on the same street as the Hanks family motorcycle dealership in Erdington, Birmingham. Roy had only just turned 18 and had been coming to the TT for many years with his father Fred, who drove sidecars from the 1950s to 1970. Now his father made him learn the course by riding round and round on a moped, in order to memorise the correct sequence of corners. However, his first outing as a competitor was not a happy one. Roy remembered:

> I hated that first TT. It scared the living daylights out of me … After my first practice on the outfit I decided that I couldn't cope with it and was ill for the rest of the week. To be honest I couldn't wait for it all to be over … In the race I recall riding down Cronk-Y-Voddy straight at next-to-nothing miles an hour on my BSA when Siggi Schauzu's passenger Horst Schneider lent across and pulled Freddie Holden's leg to 'politely' ask us to move over as we were obviously in their way.[13]

Approaching Handley's Corner with a high wall in front of him, he froze, unable to remember if it was a right turn or a left. Despite this rather less than promising start, Roy was hooked on TT racing now, and decided to buckle down to learn the course properly. The same year was also to see the TT debut of Mick Boddice, son of Bill. Through family connections Mick had secured first an apprenticeship and then a job with BSA in Birmingham. He remembered:

They called us the Birmingham BSA riders ... [Competition workshop manager] Brian Martin was always helpful with bits and pieces but there were no special parts, even if he did give us time off to go racing. The first time I could do the TT I went into his office and said, 'Can I have the last week in May and first week in June as my holidays?' And he said, 'No, but we can pay you and you can go.'[14]

Boddice was a retirement in that first race, but would soldier on with the BSA for another four years, achieving a best place of fourth in that time. Over in Germany, meanwhile, there was disharmony in the BMW camp. Helmut Fath had been out of racing for five years as he struggled to recover from a serious crash at the Nürburgring. During this time he had made a living by tuning engines for other riders, including Florian Camathias. So good was his work that he often outstripped riders on factory-prepared engines, and some resentment towards him had developed at BMW. When Fath approached them seeking support in his return to racing, they refused to assist him; humiliated, Fath vowed to develop his own engine and outfit. With assistance from Dr Peter Kuhn of Heidelberg University, and fellow engineer Horst Owesle, he began work on his project in his workshop at Ursenbach, which inspired the name URS. The engine they created was unlike anything seen before; though outwardly similar to a Gilera four-cylinder motor, the eight-valve URS was inwardly very different. It featured two separate crankshafts (set at 90 degrees) driving a common countershaft. Mounted on its right-hand end were the contact-breakers for the twin-plug ignition. Kuhn's knowledge of special valve springs enabled the URS to rev at up to 15,000rpm, which was exceptional for a 500cc four with two large valves per cylinder. Bore and stroke dimensions were 60 × 44mm and a Bosch fuel injection system was employed, the first successful use of fuel injection on a racing motorcycle. Although it was larger, heavier and had a higher centre of gravity than its arch-rival, the BMW flat twin, the higher-revving URS produced 84–88bhp compared to the BMW's 65–70bhp, which was more than enough to overcome those shortcomings. Instead of serial numbers, Fath gave names to his engines, which were called 'Emil', 'Friedrich', 'Gustav' and 'Heinrich'. 'Gustav' was the most successful, usually being reserved for qualifying and races. After testing, Fath made his first serious reappearance on the sidecar stage in 1967. He retired at the TT that year, but better results were to come.

Roy Hanks' appearance at the 1967 TT was also memorable for the wrong reasons, and proved that he still had a lot to learn, as he recalled:

> I approached Sarah's Cottage in a morning practice, braked hard and spun on the damp road. The outfit overturned. I took a chunk out of my shoulder and the fingerprints were rubbed off my fingers.[15]

Colin Seeley, meanwhile, was appearing at his last TT in 1967, having decided to retire from racing to concentrate on his motorcycle business. By now he was sporting a BMW engine, mounted in a chassis that had been built for him by TT legend Ken Sprayson (known as 'the frame man'). Sprayson worked for the Reynolds Tube Company and had access to light, high-strength manganese-molybdenum alloy steel, of the type known as '531'. The weather now dawned bright and clear on this June morning, as it always seemed to in the 1960s. Seeley recalled:

> Up at the start, the enclosure gates opened at 10am and the 158 riders and passengers, supported by their mechanics, wheeled the outfits from the overnight marquee and made final checks and adjustments before the 15-minute warm-up at 10.30am. People were pushing and shoving in all directions in an effort to get started. Onlookers wandered into the way, amongst shouts of 'out of the way', the roar of engines, the smoke, the commotion and officials trying to bring some sort of order into that small terraced paddock area. It all appeared a shambles. Suddenly the siren echoed through the area to stop engines and for competitors to assemble on the grid. Now there was no going back.[16]

Starting alongside was Seeley's friend, Helmut Fath on his super-fast URS four-cylinder machine. Fath passed them at Union Mills but Seeley managed to stay with him until the Mountain climb, when the raw power of the URS motor really began to tell and Fath pulled away. His engine failed, however, at the Bungalow on the second lap. Another front runner, Georg Auerbacher with passenger Eduard Dein, also retired on the third lap, on the approach to Ballacraine.

On only his second visit to the Isle of Man, West German Siegfried Schauzu with passenger Horst Schneider won the Diamond Jubilee 1967 sidecar TT. Fellow countryman Klaus Enders with Ralph Engelhardt was second, and in third place Colin Seeley with Liverpudlian Roy Lindsey. In addition, Seeley had helped the Greenwich Motor and Motorcycle Club take the team prize. As he stood on the rostrum, Seeley reflected on his decision to retire from racing. A true patriot, he had found it emotional to see the Union Flag raised, and he was proud of his achievements on the Isle of Man, not least in this final race when his almost worn out Rennsport engine had put him on a par with the Germans (who always had the best parts) as the first British crew home. While the race went to Siegfried Schauzu, the World Championship went to up and coming rival Klaus Enders.

In 1968, the TT organisers introduced a second sidecar race to the schedule for the first time. The 500cc race, which carried World Championship points, was now joined on the programme by a 750cc international race. This was ostensibly to give the bigger-engined British machines a chance of beating the BMW outfits, which dominated at 500cc. It also, of course, meant that a new trophy would be required, and the Middlesbrough branch of the ACU duly provided one, to be known as the Fred W. Dixon trophy in honour of their illustrious former member. Passengering Mick Potter in this race was newcomer Tony Davis, who remembered:

> The race, while it lasted, fully lived up to my expectations with a couple of unplanned incidents thrown in for good

measure. The outfits started in pairs and we were on the second rank alongside Norman Hanks and beside favourite Terry Vinicombe and Mac Hobson. Just before the off, Mac's engine spewed oil onto the road. I tried to warn Mick but he was concentrating on the flag so that as we pushed off I was unable to avoid the slippery puddle and had to take every opportunity during the next few miles to drag the sole of my boots on the tarmac to try to scrape the oil off. Then on lap two Mick braked a little too hard at Rhencullen and, hanging out for the left-hander, I was jolted forward and whacked my elbow on the road. To this day there is a piece of bone floating about in the joint. Worse, it ripped my leathers and I later had to have the arm patched at some expense.

Disaster struck on lap two while we were running fifth. As we accelerated out of Waterworks I heard a rattle and to my horror saw that the barrel nuts were coming loose. I tapped Mick's leg to draw his attention to the problem but before he could de-clutch the cylinders lifted off the crankcase and wrecked the engine.[17]

Eventual winner Terry Vinicombe should have been assured of a golden future in sidecar motorsport. A talented driver with an unassuming, quietly spoken nature, he died a few months later of an illness unrelated to racing, aged just 32.

It is easy to forget that while those at the font of the grid are making headlines and grabbing glory, further down the field are competitors who derive just as much satisfaction simply by overcoming the technical challenges that sidecar racing at the

TT presents; for many, finishing a race is a goal in itself. One of the best accounts from a journeyman racer of this era is that of George Bye who, with passenger Brian Spriggs and mechanics John Handleigh and Tony Crabb, entered the 1968 TT with a 649cc Triumph-powered machine.

Practice week for them was a typical mixture of ups and downs. Early elation at getting a feel for the course and mastering the smoothest lines gave way to disappointment as under jetting resulted in a holed piston, and an engine rebuild the following day. In that evening's practice they used a reserve engine, but the vibration that it produced proved to be intolerable. Indeed by Doran's Bend it had shaken an exhaust megaphone loose, never to be seen again, and the frame required re-welding in the aftermath. The first night of practice had led them to go up an extra tooth on the gearing and this proved to be a shrewd move, as in the final practice session before the race it helped to keep the revs down, thus protecting the engine. Every lap they had completed had been faster than the previous one, as their experience of the Mountain Course grew.

Saturday, 8 June was race day for sidecars. Although this was the first year with more than one class, the two were run concurrently. The 500cc machines were to start first at 6.00 pm, whilst the 750cc class would start five minutes afterwards. This, of course, meant that a crew could not compete in both races, and had to choose, which effectively separated the British and Germans. In the 1968 TT 500cc race Auerbacher encountered similar problems to those of earlier years; the steering went loose, the first indication of a split in the frame caused by the cornering stresses to which he was subjecting his machine. His frame broke at just about the worst spot possible – on the plunge down Bray Hill going flat out. With the chair on the right in common with other continental outfits, the racing line meant they were lucky to avoid collision with a wall and even greater disaster. Auerbacher put the blame for the accident squarely on the hard tyres. They restricted drift, which strained the frame during hard cornering.

The 500cc race win was taken by Siegfried Schauzu, with third place going to up and coming German driver Heinz Luthringshauser. With the death of Fritz Scheidegger at Mallory Park the previous year, Luthringshauser had bought the outfit he had been riding that day, and after refurbishing it used it at the TT. His British passenger for three seasons in the 1960s was Geoff Hughes, who remembered:

> The first thing he did was to take me to a garden allotment area where I practised sliding in and out of the outfit with him. Heinz rode with a left-hand chair, unlike most Continentals, as he had a wooden lower right leg ... The Germans were all tough guys, and they made me tougher too ... Georg [Auerbacher] and Heinz pronounced my name Joffrey.[18]

The partnership was not to last, however, with Hughes remembering that after three years he had had enough of Luthringshauser's arrogant attitude. Fourth place in 1968 went to Fath aboard the URS, and he would go on to take the World Championship that year. It was the first occasion since 1953 that a non-BMW-powered machine had won, and it was the only ever victory by a competitor riding a home-built machine. Runner-up in the World Championship that year was to be Auerbacher, the best-placed BMW rider. Indeed, 1968 really should have been Auerbacher's year, and it was the season in which he came closest in his career to taking the World Championship. He won the Spanish Grand Prix in Barcelona, and the Italian at Monza. In the TT he set the fastest lap of the race and had a lead of half a minute when he dropped out.

In the 750cc TT the first lap went well for Bye and Spriggs, with Tony Crabb giving them a board at the Grandstand showing they had just achieved their first ever lap under thirty minutes. By the end of the second lap they were going even faster and were holding tenth place, having passed some of the 500cc outfits as well as two of the 750s. Bye takes up the story at this point:

> After two laps, at 76.16mph, we were well inside silver replica time, which exceeded our wildest dreams. The engine was going better than ever on the third lap ... It was with renewed determination that we began our last half-lap, feeling sure this was our day. As we came out from the avenue of trees that precedes Milntown Cottage, the motor started missing; and spluttered to a halt just before the first left-hander. I didn't actually cry, but I was very near to it.
>
> Brian was leaping around, checking things desperately. We had no plug spanner and couldn't check the spark. Ignition leads seemed OK. Compression appeared normal (a holed piston was foremost in our minds); all the

carburettor connections were intact. It must have been five minutes before it was noticed that the fuel supply pipe to the carburettors was empty. During this time practically all the outfits we'd overtaken came buzzing by. Brian literally flew into the sidecar nose to discover a broken wire connection to the battery. Tearing at the plastic insulating cover with his teeth, he rapidly made a repair. The engine refused to start when we started pushing. After a couple of attempts, and feeling utterly dejected and exhausted, it was realized that the switch was still off, and the fuel pipe still empty. It was a case of more haste less speed, but eventually we got away.

We stopped again on the Mountain when the temporary repair came loose again. Brian secured it once more and we attempted to blast home. I don't think we've ever come down the Mountain so fast, but our lap time was 34m 53.0s, bringing our race average down to 72.08mph, and our final placing to 14th.[19]

Returning to the Grandstand, there was jubilation among the group, by now joined by wives and girlfriends, that they had done it. Sitting in the marquee after the race, sharing stories of mishap with other crews, with the excited chatter nearly raising the roof, was one of the best moments of the week, exceeded only later that evening when they learned that they had achieved the fastest bronze replica.

Roy Hanks' older brother Norman was by now making his name at the TT, having started racing a couple of years earlier, and this year's 750cc event would give him his best result, a second place. Many agree that of the two brothers Norman had the more competitive temperament, and Roy himself rated his brother as someone who never fulfilled his true potential:

> Norman was a brilliant driver. He worked at the BSA factory in his younger days ... He went off to the States ... And came back with lots of fancy ideas from the American scene. It was he who came up with the bright orange and black colour scheme. He said, 'It's all colourful out there, you've got to be seen.' So we devised a new colour scheme that Norman and I both rode with. Norman packed up racing as he said he wasn't prepared to ride uncompetitive machinery against the likes of the BMWs.[20]

Between 1967 and 1969 Norman had a female passenger, Rose Arnold, who the Hanks brothers had met some time earlier at Mallory Park when she was passengering for other drivers. Rose would eventually go on to marry Roy, but she made TT history with Norman by becoming the first woman to stand on the TT podium. Rose remembers:

> My interest in motorcycles came about when I was young, my dad had three motorcycles, my brother also. I've been around bikes most of my life. The first go I had as a passenger was on a scramble outfit on an airfield; I was hooked. I decided I wanted to passenger. In 1965 a friend, Ken West, had a sidecar outfit, the first ride I had was at a sprint, we finished 2nd. I rode passenger for Freddie Wallis for a season, but my main ambition was to ride

in the TT. In 1967 I got my big break when Roy Hanks (now my husband) visited me at home and in general conversation mentioned that Norman, his eldest brother, was looking for a passenger for the season and the TT. I jumped at the chance as I knew Norman was one of the top sidecar drivers of his time along with Chris Vincent, etc. March 1967 was my first race meeting with Norman and I obviously wanted to create a good impression. The track was Mallory Park and we were on the start line waiting for the off. It was a push start in those days and as the engine fired up Norman brought his leg over and kicked my shoulder; off the back I went. I thought to myself what a great start to the season. I got back on and we finished 2nd, not bad considering my mishap.

Later that year, at the 1967 TT, we took part in the 500cc Sidecar Race, unfortunately we had a few problems, finishing 27th.[21]

The following year was their best result together, and she speaks eloquently of her feelings at the time. While she did not think of her achievement as striking a blow for women's equality, she acknowledges that she did realise that something special had happened:

(Finishing 2nd) made me the first woman ever to stand on the Winner's Rostrum. It was like a dream come true. I was on cloud nine and can't remember much about it except that at the Awards Presentation the other sidecar crews presented me with a bouquet. The same year ...

> I was taken to Hillberry to be presented to Prince Phillip, which was a great honour ... all those that finished behind were genuinely pleased for us. At the presentation Chris Vincent presented me with a lovely bouquet from the competitors. I also had a trophy from the Women's International Motorcycle Association of America ... I passengered for Roy at the TT in 1970, finishing 7th in the first race but blowing an engine in the second. It's amazing how the techniques of two drivers are so different. I was meeting Roy in the chair on left-handers as he got over for the corner sooner than Norman used to; but remember, sidecars had front exits and you had to work from back to front very quickly. When you ride with one driver for a while you think alike and tend to know what they are going to do next ...[22]

Less well known, but proving that women passengers were widely accepted within the sidecar world, was Dane Rowe, who competed at the TT in 1968 and 1969. A keen motorcyclist from an early age, Dane had passengered on an ad hoc basis at a number of British meetings in the mid-1960s. Then she found herself at the TT when BMW rider Bill Copson needed a passenger. He asked her if she would like to join him but, apprehensive, she told him she had no equipment. However, his son soon found her leathers and a helmet. Her most vivid memory was of taking Ballaugh Bridge as passenger to Colin Bird in 1969:

> [I remember] hoping we wouldn't lose the sidecar nose entirely. The plexiglass screen of the sidecar nose had

cracked and the vibration had started to spread so much, that it split the sidecar nose floor (the 'pan') as well, so that started to dangle off. Normally that wouldn't be a problem, but that's where the battery was, so the last one and a half laps of the race was spent with me holding the battery in place, as half of the floor beneath the battery was broken off and held in place only by about 2 inches of fibreglass.[23]

Confounding the cynics, West Germany's Siegfried Schauzu romped away with the winner's laurels in the 1969 750cc sidecar TT – twice in sixteen hours! Some said he had been lucky to win the 1967 and 1968 500cc sidecar TTs, taking over after others had retired. But this time, 'Sideways Sid' as he was affectionately known to British fans, left no room for doubt. He led the three-lap race for every one of its 113.2 miles to notch a new race record of 89.83mph – 0.72mph faster than Chris Vincent's 1968 lap record with a 650cc BSA. After that, no one questioned that Schauzu had earned his victory – that is until the ACU disqualified him! The organisation said that he had failed to stop his engine when, goggles smothered with dead flies, he and passenger Horst Schneider had picked up fresh pairs at their pit as they started the final lap. He appealed, and the ACU accepted that there was insufficient evidence that he had kept his engine running so he was reinstated. Chris Vincent's BSA stopped with transmission problems on the last lap but Peter Brown was runner-up his 750cc BSA twin ahead of Bill Currie on a 650cc Triumph. A newcomer, he was aiming only to finish and had not arranged for signals, so he was astonished to be ushered into the winners' enclosure.

Of the sixty-nine starters, only thirty-three went the full distance. Klaus Enders beat his Isle of Man jinx – and suspected sabotage – to win the 500cc sidecar TT. Foiled by a broken con-rod with 4 miles to go the previous year, he led all the way this time to notch a race record of 92.48mph. He won despite being forced to strip and rebuild his BMW's engine on the eve of the race, when he and Georg Auerbacher both found sand (or something similar) in their combustion chambers. Enders' mechanic Dieter Busch said:

> Someone put abrasive powder in the carburettor intake. It was sucked into the engine and scoured a piston.[24]

Auerbacher's engine was more extensively damaged. He alleged that a spark plug had been removed and the powder poured in. As a result, both had to weigh in late, but Auerbacher was less fortunate than Enders. Lying third for a time, he stopped briefly on the first lap and then retired on the second, suspecting dirt in his BMW's fuel line. In frustration at his lack of success in previous years, for the 1969 TT Auerbacher had built a shorter-wheelbase frame, hoping that this would allow for a greater degree of drifting. It might well have done, but once again he was the author of his undoing – it later transpired that it was not dirt but a piece of fibreglass from a poorly repaired fuel tank that came adrift and found its way into a petrol feed pipe, starving the engine.

As expected, the race was completely dominated by West Germans. Early challenger to Enders was Helmut Fath on his home-built four-cylinder URS. But as the race progressed so his pace slackened, letting 750cc winner Siegfried Schauzu (BMW) into second place. Enders reported a trouble-free race, but criticised the course:

> Every year it gets bumpier. This year it was very bad in Ramsey, but I am happy to have won at last.[25]

For 1970 on the Isle of Man Auerbacher's biggest concern was with his clutch, but he overcame problems in this area to finish sixth in the 500cc race. His run of mechanical bad luck was coming to an end, and back on the Island in 1971 he recorded his first win in nearly ten years of competing, despite a slipping clutch. He also posted the fastest lap and finished second in the 500cc event two days later, a mere 5.4 seconds behind Siegfried Schauzu. Sadly, Auerbacher's racing career was ended the following year by a serious crash at the thirteenth Milestone during TT practice. After his front brake locked he went head first over a wall and collided with a tree. Passenger Peter Rutherford was only slightly injured but Auerbacher compressed three vertebrae and suffered head injuries, remaining in a coma at Noble's Hospital for almost four weeks. When he awoke he had no memory of the crash and refused at first to believe that he was still in the Isle of Man, thinking that the 'MN' number plates he could see from his hospital window were those of Mindelheim, his home district in Bavaria. He suffered frequent headaches for much of the remainder of his life, which made prolonged concentration (and working) difficult, but he remained philosophical, and above all grateful to Josef Ried the mechanic, who in his view had sacrificed seven years of his youth to support his World Championship dreams.

By contrast the most successful West German sidecar driver from this era, indeed the most successful German motorcycle racer ever, was Klaus Enders. Enders, who was born in 1937 in Wetzlar about 40 miles north of Frankfurt, started his racing career in the early 1960s. Initially he had competed both as a solo rider and sidecar driver simultaneously, and in 1963 he won the 500cc German junior solo championship, followed in 1964 by the overall German 500cc championship. However, the cost of competing across the board forced him to make a decision, and in 1966 he chose to focus upon sidecar racing. His first sidecar World Championship came in 1967, with a second title in 1969 and a third in 1970. For the 1971 season, Enders withdrew from sidecar competition to try to break into four-wheeled racing, but was unsuccessful.

Having been humiliated in the sidecar World Championship by Fath in 1968, BMW suffered the same fate in 1971. This time it was at the hands of Horst Owesle and Peter Rutherford, who were using the same immensely powerful URS outfit that Fath had built. Sensing the threat that the now upgraded URS represented, for the 1972 season the Munich manufacturer was, not surprisingly, eager to bring the World Championship title back to Bavaria. For this purpose the factory promised extensive support to the already successful Grand Prix trio of Enders (driver), Ralf Englehardt (passenger) and Dieter Busch (sponsor, constructor and engine tuner). The trio already had a record of success, as their three previous World Championships in 1967, 1969 and 1970 attested. Dieter Busch deserves special mention as probably the person who did most to develop and prolong the life of the BMW flat-twin engine in sidecars. Among his modifications were larger intake valves, and lightening of rotating and moving parts such as pistons. He experimented with different sizes of carburettor, bell mouths, intake and exhaust pipe length. He found that a longer exhaust with a more open megaphone produced an increase in power of around 9bhp. He also discovered that a wet sump lubrication system partially starved some of the bearings of oil, whereas conversion of engines to a dry sump system, with resultant lower engine position in the frame, improved the oil supply. His greatest contribution, however, was development of the centre bearing engine, and so great was his intervention that by 1974 his power units would contain hardly any unmodified parts and would be known as Busch-BMW motors; indeed the 1974 constructor's World Championship was to be awarded in this name.

In 1972, following his lack of success in car racing, Enders took up the Bavarian firm's offer of support, and with Dieter Busch began to develop a machine capable of retaking the sidecar world title. Busch reached deep into his bag of tricks and built a delicate, one-piece, monocoque chassis using aircraft steel only 1mm thick. To the standard BMW 500cc flat twin Rennsport engine he also introduced his innovative additional third bearing at the centre, and its own ignition system. This motor, when tuned, produced 67bhp. The wheels and brake system were developed in parallel, in the workshop of Klaus Enders. Because he thought very little of disc brakes, Enders favoured a double-duplex drum brake system, and constructed his own hubs for the wheels. Due to the fact that BMW's commitment to support them had come quite late in the day, it was not until the third World Championship race of the 1972 season, at the Salzburgring on 14 May, that they were ready to compete. They had already missed the West German and French rounds, which went to Siegfried Schauzu and Heinz Luthringshauser respectively. However, it had been worth the wait, for Enders and Englehardt took victory in that first outing in Austria.

The next meeting was the Isle of Man TT. Here Enders and Englehardt were less successful, retiring in both the 500cc and 750cc races, but they went on to take three more victories with wins at the Dutch TT at Assen, the Belgian round at Spa and the Czechoslovakian Grand Prix at Brno. With seventy-two points, and a nine-point lead over nearest rival Luthringshauser, it was enough to give them the world title. Using the same outfit, they went into the 1973 campaign as reigning World Champions. This was to be a historic season in Grand Prix terms, for out of seven starts, Enders and Englehardt won them all, giving them their fifth world title and BMW their eighteenth.

They came to the Isle of Man TT that year as favourites, and threw down a gauntlet to their rivals when in practice they unofficially broke the lap record. The first sidecar outing of the meeting was the 750cc race on the Saturday and conditions were less than ideal. A still-wet road was slowly drying under a clearing sky and with a warm breeze, and the packed field was thinned by a number of machines that flatly refused to fire up. As the race got under way, Siegfried Schauzu ('Sideways Sid') intended to show Enders that he would not be having things all his own way. Schauzu, who was also BMW-powered, actually caught him at the Bungalow, and kept the pressure on right through those first two laps. The roadsides were littered with British riders whose outfits had failed, but the two Teutonic Knights jostled for position, urged on by shouts of '*schnell, schnell*' from the many German spectators who lined the course. By the third lap, however, it was noticeable that Schauzu's pace was slowing and Enders was able to draw away from him. Indeed he was on blistering form and took the chequered flag with over a minute to spare. It was an incredible performance with a new lap record and a new race time and race speed being set.

Even greater things were to follow, however, on Monday, 4 June 1973, for this was the date for the 500cc event, the one that counted for World Championship points. For the fans soaking up the sun on the banks and hedges as they waited for the race to start, there was only one possible outcome. Enders was clear favourite to win. Only one man had done the sidecar 'double' up to this point, his rival Siegfried Schauzu, but Enders was set to join him in that exclusive club. Schauzu for his part was under no illusion just how far out of contention he really was now, telling reporters:

Enders is too fast for me. I know. So I plan to go for second place.[26]

The weather for this race was ideal with a dry road and a gentle breeze blowing. For Enders and Englehardt, however, it was a bad start, for it took them 30 yards of hard pushing to get the outfit to fire up. Nevertheless, Enders quickly started carving his way through the eight competitors on the road ahead of him, bypassing Schauzu as he did so, and by Ballacraine was in the lead on time. By Ballaugh it was thought that he might well be on course for the first 100mph sidecar lap, so fast was he going. Rocketing through Ramsey, he was leading on the road as well by the time he reached the Bungalow, and held an incredible forty-eight-second lead over second-place man Schauzu at this point; with Brits cast aside once more, by this stage in the race it was German machines in first, second, third, and fourth places. The real battle was now between BMW power and its up and coming rival König, as Rolf Steinhausen tried to get in on the action. The first lap was a new record set by Enders, and he powered through the second in fine style. Schauzu was by now one minute forty seconds astern, and nothing short of a major misfortune to Enders would hand him the race. By the third lap, engine preservation was becoming Enders' main concern, but even so he set another lap record on his final circuit. The *TT Special* noted:

> Last lap excitement continued with Enders heading for his first double TT victory and more World Championship points. Everywhere he gets the acclaim of the spectators. This acclaim is more than well deserved for he is on the peak of his skill and he is a delight to watch. With 45 World Championship points already in the bag another 15 look like putting him in an unassailable position for the world crown.[27]

As the West German national anthem *'Deutschland Über Alles'* drifted across the Grandstand and paddock following the garlanding ceremony, the sun was setting on one of the finest days of racing in the long history of the TT, a glorious day for German motorsport, and certainly one of the best days in the annals of sidecar racing on the Isle of Man.

In 1974 the BMW factory retired from sidecar Grand Prix racing, and so Enders and Englehardt competed using the same machine but under the HBM banner. The abbreviation represented the name of their main sponsor, the Frankfurt BMW dealer Gert Heukerott (HBM standing for 'Heukerott Busch Motor'.) Again in 1974, despite reduced BMW support and the growing threat from Berlin-based factory König, whose machinery was growing in popularity, they again took the world title, only two points ahead of the runners-up Schwärzel and Kleis on a two-stroke König. In the Isle of Man that year, the two sidecar races were won by Siegfried Schauzu and Heinz Luthringshauser respectively. However, it was the swansong for the BMW flat twin engine, for at the TT and elsewhere it would be briefly eclipsed by the König, before it too was outclassed in the sidecar field by Yamaha TZ engines.

With the collapse of British firm BSA in 1973, the supply of these engines and spare parts soon also began to dry up. For a while the powerful König engine seemed to offer an alternative, but as many British riders such as Mick Boddice (after a brief flirtation with a Kawasaki motor) discovered, the engine was extremely porous and leaked water constantly. This was fine in a speedboat for which the engine was designed, but not ideally suited to sidecars. Boddice persevered with the König at the TT for three years, but all he got for his trouble was a string of DNFs and a best finish of twenty-fourth place. By 1977, like most of the smart riders he was on Yamaha engines. He was offered support at the time from sponsor Dennis Trollope, but this came with the proviso that he would also need to sign a deal with Castrol. Out of a misguided sense of loyalty to his existing sponsor Shell, Boddice turned down the deal, and Trollope put his backing behind up-and-coming star Jock Taylor. Twelve months later, Shell pulled out of major competition sponsorship, leaving Boddice to wonder what might have been if he had accepted the Trollope offer.

In February 1974, Joe and Alma Rocheleau received the offer of a lifetime. They were contacted by the Competition Director of the American Motorcycle Association, who told them that because they were the top American sidecar team in the Sidecar Racers Association, they were to be given the only invitation the association had for a pairing to enter the Isle of Man Tourist Trophy races. The only slight snag was that this was an 'invitation' that did not guarantee a starting place for the race, or include sponsorship. Joe and Alma would have to finance everything themselves. However, this was the chance to make a dream come true and they jumped at it.

Late May and early June are considered to be summer time by Americans, but they discovered that in Britain around the time of the TT races the weather can be decidedly less than summery. Even more than by the gloomy weather, Joe and Alma's spirits were dampened further when they arrived at their hotel on the Isle of Man to discover that their BSA-powered sidecar rig was still a hundred miles away, across the Irish Sea in Liverpool. Joe had to fly back to Liverpool to see what the situation was, and to find a solution to the problem of the unmoving sidecar racer crate. It turned out that the crate that the sidecar rig was in was too wide to fit into the hold of the cargo aircraft that was to transport it. This called for some lateral thinking. Would Joe have to unpack and reassemble the sidecar rig to ride it to the Isle of Man Steam Packet Company pier? No he would not, although he was prepared to do so, and in all probability back in 1970s Britain the local constabulary would have either turned a blind eye, or more likely helped him to accomplish it. It was a little lateral thinking that avoided all that drama. Joe knew that the crate containing the bike could be tipped up on its side without risk of damage to the bike. With the crate tipped on its edge it fitted neatly into the cargo hold of the aircraft, and was able to wing its way to the Isle of Man.

On the approach to Ramsey Hairpin, Joe and Alma went from full throttle to hard braking, timing it just right in order to get their speed down enough to make the almost 180-degree turn. As they approached the corner, the marshal was not signalling danger, so as they rounded the bend, Joe opened the throttle and suddenly things came unglued at racing speed. Before they knew it the bike had snapped around and flipped Alma over Joe in an almost graceful arc, knocking Joe off the bike as well. The stunned pair lost no time, both were OK, the bike landed on its wheels and was still in working order, so it was back into the saddle, a push start to get the engine going and throttle open to make up the lost seconds. It would not be until the second lap that Joe and Alma found out what had really happened. Approaching the Ramsey Hairpin for the second time, the flagman was now enthusiastically waving to indicate 'oil on the track', something he should have been doing on Joe and Alma's first lap! Their names went into the history of the Isle of Man TT, finishing in a respectable thirtieth place, after starting at seventy-sixth. Not only that, but they were and still are the only American husband and wife team to compete in the Isle of Man TT sidecar event.

In 1975 the international race went up from 750cc to 1,000cc. Among the overseas competitors that year was Alex Campbell, the most successful sidecar racer in Australia, who had heard that speeds were faster at the TT and wanted to try his hand on the Isle of Man. The owner of Campbell Yamaha, a dealership in Mount Gambier, South Australia, he was also a talented engineer, building his own frames and pioneering the development of Yamaha 350cc two-strokes in sidecar racing in the southern hemisphere. Like a number of others at the time, he was experimenting with bolting two 350s onto a single crankshaft to make a 700cc engine that was incredibly powerful. He finished a creditable seventh in the 500cc event that year, and returned to the Isle of Man in 1976, when he managed sixth in the 1,000cc international race. His success continued at the by-now revived Australian TT that year, where he took an easy win in the sidecar race. Campbell, however, was to be killed just four years later in a smash while racing in the Australian sidecar championship at Adelaide International Raceway.

To take the Yamaha engine down from a 700cc capacity to 500cc was a relatively straightforward procedure; it was first necessary to remove the 350cc heads, barrels and pistons. Two sets of 250cc barrels, heads and pistons were then fitted in their place, but the heads, being meant for two separate 250cc twins, fitted very closely together. In fact, they actually overlapped, and to prevent this it was necessary to remove excess metal on the inside edges of the heads. Sometimes barrels and heads would need to go on and off several times before a suitable gap between them was achieved. Another frequently encountered snag was the right-hand carburettor fouling the clutch housing, due to the absence of reed valve ducts on the barrels. By reducing the fibre manifold on this cylinder to half its normal thickness, it was possible to get the float chamber just clear. The difference in length of the inlet duct did not affect the running to any noticeable degree. In the 500cc form, however, the engine was notoriously harder to push start, and when running the lack of power was noticeable below 8,000rpm.

Milton Mitchinson was a passenger at the 1976 TT, with driver Ken Blacklock. After an eventful Practice Week that included an engine destroyed in dramatic fashion by the chain picking up a stone, which over-tensioned it, men and machine were ready for the main event. Monday of Race Week saw the first sidecar race, and in scrutineering that morning another minor problem was identified in the form of a small hole in the fuel tank. With the leak quickly fixed with Araldite, the machine was passed and the waiting began until 1pm, when it was time to change into leathers. Mitchinson continues:

> At the pits, having seen the clan to the grandstand, we start the warming up period. Tension is building up. Looking around, the effect can be seen, some sit away on their own looking thoughtful, others laugh a little too easily. But some are apparently unaffected. Mac Hobson has his usual grin for everyone, Luthringshauser is telling

us that his BMW is 1953 outside but new inside and Greasley has his serious look for most (he doesn't smile much, that boy!)

The 'Stop Engines' sign is up. Silence. The first outfits are being pushed onto the Glencrutchery Road. Our number is 67, which means starting 5½ minutes behind the leaders, so there is no hurry for us to get out there. Once we have established ourselves in the queue, nervousness subsides. This happens to me every time at the TT. It probably has something to do with being occupied ...

It's 2.30 and the first engines burst into life. In a minute or two we are within three or four rows of the line. Down come our visors and Jim checks that they are secure. A quick 'Good luck' and he is off to his pit position. We stand alone on the line as our companion outfit is a non-starter. The miniature flag falls and we push away. The engine is reluctant but eventually comes into its power band. We accelerate.[28]

As the lap progressed, the dark side of racing reared its ugly head:

A slight jump and a rise in revs tells me we have passed the Halfway House pub and I look up, waiting for the Highlander to arrive. There it is, and the yellow flag is out. Ken slows the plot. I glance up and there is a large column of smoke showing over the trees at Greeba Castle. Passing the Highlander, more yellow flags and the first signs of a serious accident – some debris on the road. By now we are travelling very steadily and, cresting the rise, see the rest. One figure is lying by the right-hand kerb, his condition obvious. Further on two or three marshals are attending his mate who has his head raised and looks to be conscious. The outfit has gone into the straw bales at Greeba and they are alight for about 25 yards. We are now at the rear of about five outfits proceeding relatively slowly through Appledene, everyone affected by the scenes behind.[29]

Mitchinson admitted that the sight of the fatal accident at Greeba, in which West German driver Walter Wörner was killed, had unsettled him and he had difficulty concentrating for the rest of the lap, but by the second half of the race his focus had returned. He and his driver finished thirteenth in the event, earning bronze replicas. On the following Wednesday they went one better, achieving twelfth in the 1,000cc race. Thus ended just over a week of hard work, excitement, a sense of achievement and every emotion possible. As with perhaps a third of the entry, Mitchinson and Blacklock were Yamaha powered. In 1976, Mac Hobson and Mick Burns aboard a Yamaha TZ-powered machine took the 1,000cc sidecar race at the TT, ahead of BMW-powered Schauzu. It was the first sidecar win at the TT for the Japanese marque, and it set the pattern for the coming decade when Yamaha motors would dominate both sidecar classes.

Chapter 4

Dawn of Japan

In the 1960s, the sidecar events at the TT had largely been dominated by German and Swiss riders on BMW-engined outfits. However, by the mid-1970s British drivers had begun a fightback, which was to a large extent due to the arrival of the Yamaha TZ750 engine. It was affordable, easily obtainable, reliable and worked well in a sidecar outfit. The man who would take this engine, together with a Windle chassis, into the TT history books was George O'Dell, when in 1977, together with passenger Kenny Arthur, he broke the 100mph barrier for sidecars in the Isle of Man, in the same year that he secured the sidecar World Championship. It was one of the most memorable events in sidecar history and O'Dell, though his TT career was short, was one of the most colourful characters that the sport has produced. This is the story of the battle for the ton – and beyond!

George O'Dell was born in Hemel Hempstead in 1945, and worked as an engineer at Kents Brushworks. He had been a leather-clad rocker in his youth, until an accident on his road bike lessened his interest in two-wheelers, and instead he begin to consider three. O'Dell's involvement in sidecar racing quickly grew. He made his Isle of Man debut in 1970, but the 1971 TT was almost his last, when a bad crash put both O'Dell and his passenger in hospital. Many of his early rides were on BSA machinery, before converting to König two-stroke technology like a number of his contemporaries. O'Dell's fiery character made him determined to make his mark on the Grand Prix scene, and in 1975 his attitude made an impression on Eric May, a Berkshire businessman who became a major sponsor. It was May who purchased for O'Dell his first TZ engine, acquired through a Swiss Yamaha importer.

Having the Yamaha engine alone, however, was not enough to bring success. O'Dell used it with a chassis made by one of the greatest constructors in British sidecar history, Terry Windle. A machinist by trade, Windle started racing solos in 1961, with his first race being at Rhydymwyn in Wales. His solo career was short-lived, however, as he soon took up sidecar racing. This led to him building his own chassis in his garage before opening up his own workshop in the village of Thurgoland. His sidecar chassis-building career spanned over forty years, and even after officially retiring in 2008 he continued to build bikes again in the garage behind his house. Through this time his chassis won five World Championships with riders George O'Dell, Jock Taylor, Darren Dixon and twice with Steve Abbott. O'Dell began using the Windle outfit almost by accident. He had sold his previous machine in 1975 and had intended to build his own hub-centred steering outfit. However, he did not complete it in time for the 1976 season, and so purchased the Windle as a stopgap. Although unintended, it was a good move – as O'Dell later commented, Windle machinery was ideally suited for the bumpy TT circuit. However, 1976 was not a great year for O'Dell at the TT. His regular passenger was badly injured in a collision with a wall, and he returned home from the event with nothing. At the same time, however, he was making progress and gaining experience in Grands Prix events in Europe, and acquired a new passenger in the form of Kenny Arthur, a maintenance engineer with Lever Brothers on Merseyside. For the 1977 season O'Dell put all he had into the purchase of a Seymaz chassis, which would be his main outfit. However, the trusty Windle remained his backup, and with the Seymaz damaged at Cadwell Park in spring 1977, it was to take centre stage at that year's TT. Unlike the previous year, in which it had appeared in the yellow and green livery of main sponsor BP, this time it was in the distinctive yellow and red of Shell. So highly was O'Dell regarded by this stage, that the rival oil company had made him a financial offer that he simply could not refuse. Passenger Kenny Arthur remembered:

> The Windle was a very stable bike, particularly around the Isle of Man. It was well-proven … Lots of people had used them and you felt very confident on the bike. It was one of those bikes you could change direction on it and not feel endangered in any way – and nicely put together, it was really well engineered. Compared to the bikes today I don't suppose it was, but it just felt right. It felt very right. The circuit was a lot bumpier then, and some of the corners were a lot tighter, but the bike was good … It was a four-cylinder, two-stroke Yamaha, 750cc, which was the same engine that we used for Grands Prix, only you put 250 cylinders and pistons and exhausts on it, which took it down to a 500 for Grands Prix. Grands Prix were always 500cc at that particular time, and internationals were

Above: This rare image shows the start of a sidecar TT looking from the scoreboard. The year may be 1923, as there is no Mercury trophy visible above the scoreboard. However, what appears to be the RAC trophy is just visible on the left. (Author's Collection)

Right: Freddie Dixon, inventor of the banking sidecar, and winner of the first sidecar TT in 1923. (Author's Collection)

Below: The 1923 Dixon banking sidecar as it exists today, housed at the Milntown Collection on the Isle of Man. (Author's Collection)

1923 SIDECARISTS

Happy and exciting memories were being recalled in Douglas this week by two men who rode together as rider and passenger in the first sidecar T.T. event—held over the Mountain course—in 1923.

They are Mr Alex Fraser and Mr A. E. Taylor (seen together in the picture taken after Wednesday's sidecar race).

Both are around, as they put it, "the 60 mark," and have been keeping in touch with the T.T. events ever since that day 34 years ago when they joined the enthusiastic band of riders and passengers in what was then still a "strange and gruelling experience."

Their machine was an O.E.C. (Osborn Engineering Company) and they maintain that the present ones must be a deal more comfortable "compared with the old rigid frames."

They did not win the race in 1923, but finished the course in style, despite many setbacks. Their first came at Kirk Michael when one of the wheels of the sidecar came off. Round about Governor's Bridge they ran into another bit of trouble, but after minor repairs, sailed on to finish all right. Proudly, they say "It was a great machine and a fast one."

That year — 1923 — Freddy Dixon won the 113¼ miles race on a Douglas, at a speed of 53.15 m.p.h. His time was 2 hrs. 7 mins. 48 secs. Fastest lap was put up by H. Langman on a Scott, with a speed of 54.69 m.p.h.

Mr Fraser was riding an O.E.C. solo in the Junior event in 1923, and after an introduction, volunteered to act as passenger in the sidecar race with Mr Taylor.

The latter lives at Bromsgrove, Worcestershire, and Mr Fraser's home is at Timperley, in Cheshire.

Above left: A contemporary illustration of Harry Langman (No. 59) aboard a Scott outfit, in the 1923 sidecar TT race. (Author's Collection)

Above right: The bronze replica awarded to Arthur Kinrade for third place in the 1925 sidecar TT race. (Courtesy of Vanda Murray)

Left: A newspaper report from the 1950s featuring two of the 1923 'Sidecar men'. (Author's Collection)

Right: A BMW poster announcing the new lap record set at the TT in 1955. (Courtesy of BMW Group Classic)

Below: Stan Dibben and Cyril Smith at the 1956 sidecar TT. (Courtesy of Mark Dibben)

GERMANS "WALK AWAY" WITH SIDECAR RACE

Hillebrand 1st, Schneider 2nd, Camathias 3rd

Winner's Time: 1h. 30m. 3.4s.
Speed: 71.89 m.p.h.

RECORD LAP OF 72.55 M.P.H. BY MAN WHO LED THE FIELD

The Start, Wednesday.

GERMANY won the Sidecar International Race over the Clypse circuit to-day, and also the Manufacturers' Team Prize.

It was a repeat win for F. Hillebrand (passenger M. Grunwald). He took 1 hour 30 minutes 3.4 seconds for the race, an average speed of 71.89 m.p.h.

To Hillebrand also went the honour of creating a new lap record—time 8 minutes 55.4 seconds; speed 72.55 m.p.h.

From the word "go" he was chased by Schneider (passenger H. Strauss) driving another B.M.W., who finished second.

It was Germany's race from the start.

Hillebrand—fastest man in practice—got into the lead, and stayed there, lap after lap.

It was Hillebrand who alone lowered the lap record. That was set up by his German colleague W. Noll in 1955 in 9 mins., speed 71.93 m.p.h. In the fourth lap Hillebrand took 8 mins. 55. 4secs., to average 72.55 m.p.h.

British hopes received a setback when "Pip" Harris failed to complete his fourth circuit. Prior to that he had been going extraordinarily well—though not fast enough to catch the Germans. Cyril Smith and Bill Boddice also went out in the last stage of the race.

The Sidecar "T.T." This was how they rounded Parkfield Corner on their first circuit—Hillebrand, Schneider and Camathias. It was their finishing order, too. They gained 1st, 2nd and 3rd places, with the team prize for B.M.W.'s.

Above: A 1957 newspaper report shows sidecars making the hard right-hand turn at Parkfield Corner on the Clypse Course. (Author's Collection)

Below: 1963 TT start line, Florian Camathias (number 3) roars away followed by Bill Boddice (number 4). (Courtesy of Ken Sprayson)

Right: Bill Boddice (right) receives assistance with his Norton-Watsonian outfit from son Mick at the 1964 TT. The increasing unreliability of the engine would lead him to switch to BSA power the following year. (Courtesy of Ken Sprayson)

Below: Auerbacher and Helm (number 3) leave the start line alongside Gilera-mounted Camathias at the 1964 TT. (Courtesy of Ken Sprayson)

Above left: Camathias on the Gilera leaps Ballaugh Bridge, 1964. However, the Italian motor would not last the distance. (Author's Collection)

Above right: Max Deubel and Emil Hoerner with their BMW outfit at the 1965 TT. Heinz Luthringshauser stands behind. (Courtesy of Ken Sprayson)

Below: Deubel and Emil Hoerner in action at Governor's Dip and heading for victory in 1964. Deubel never fully adopted the 'kneeler' chassis, as can be seen here. (Courtesy of Ken Sprayson)

Above left: At the 1965 TT a new sign appeared on the course prohibiting sidecars from overtaking on the narrow approach to Ballaugh Bridge, after an incident the previous year. Shortly beyond the bridge another sign indicated that the restriction was lifted. (Author's Collection)

Above right: Rose Arnold and Norman Hanks at the 1968 TT. (Courtesy of Julie Hanks-Elliott)

Below: Siegfried Schauzu at the Mallory post-TT meeting with the ACU Mercury trophy, 1967. (Courtesy of Lothar Mildebrath)

Helmut Fath aboard the URS outfit, 1969. The engine was especially powerful on the Mountain climb. (Courtesy of Ken Sprayson)

Left: Auerbacher and Hahn on their way to victory in the 1971 750cc TT. (Courtesy of Josef Ried)

Below: Siegfried Schauzu with Horst Schneider, pulling away from Quarter Bridge at the 1969 TT. They took the 750cc race, but the 500cc went to Klaus Enders in his World Championship campaign. (Courtesy of Ken Sprayson)

Above: Dick Greasley and passenger Cliff Holland (who would go on to be World Champion with O'Dell) in 1975. Note the baseball boots almost universally worn by passengers in the 1970s. (Courtesy of Ken Sprayson)

Below: Mick Boddice and Dave Loach in the paddock at the 1974 TT. The König-powered outfit failed in both races. (Courtesy of Ken Sprayson)

Left: A thoughtful George O'Dell on the start line in 1977, with his Shell-sponsored outfit. (Courtesy of Ken Sprayson)

Below: Mac Hobson and Stuart Collins (front) with Rolf Biland and Kenny Williams (blue hats) and Kalauch and Steinhausen (red hats) following the 1977 Sidecar B race. (Courtesy of Ken Sprayson)

Above: Rolf Biland with his Seymaz outfit at the 1978 TT. Passenger Kenny Williams stands behind. (Courtesy of Ken Sprayson)

Below: Jock Taylor and Benga Johannson after success at the 1980 TT. (Courtesy of Ken Sprayson)

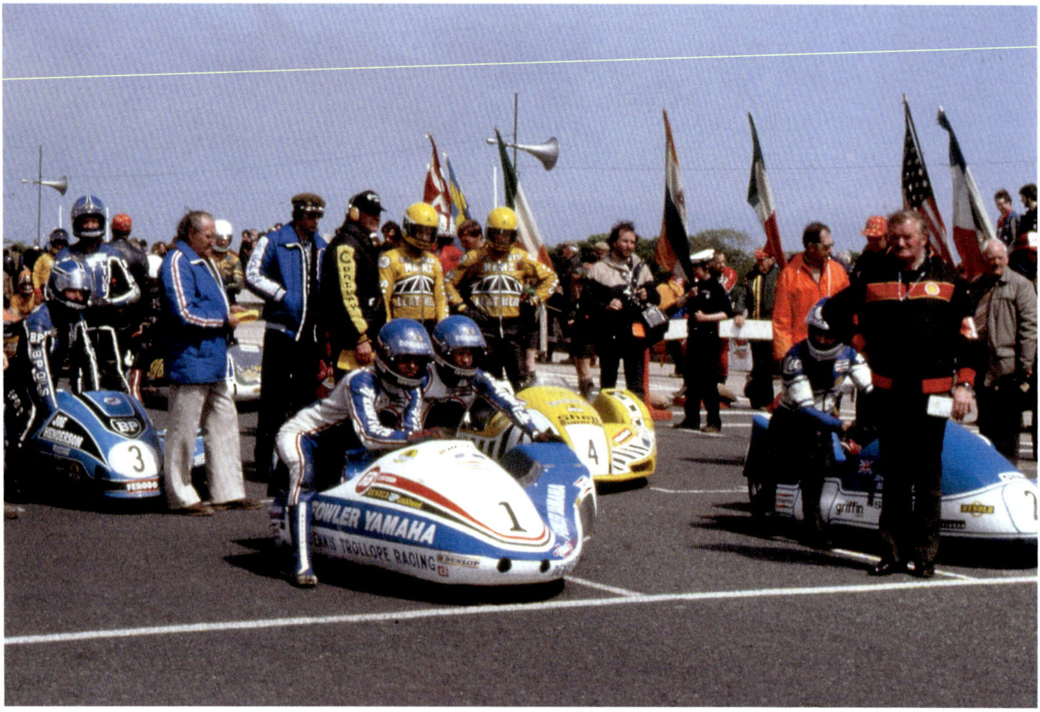

Above: Jock Taylor and Benga Johannson on the start line during the 1981 TT. Behind are Trevor Ireson/Clive Pollington and Dick Greasley/Stewart Atkinson (Courtesy of Ken Sprayson)

Below left: The 1986 sidecar TT Champion Warwick Newman with the RAC Trophy, awarded for most points over the two legs. At this time it was possible to be TT sidecar champion without actually winning either race. (Courtesy of Stourbridge News)

Below right: Dave Saville and Nick Roche at the 1990 TT. (Author's Collection)

STOURBRIDGE News

Just Champion!

Stourbridge company secretary Warwick Newman became part of the Isle of Man TT folklore by winning the 1,000 cc sidecar championship. Together with his "Chairman" Eddie Yarker, Newman lapped the famous 37½ mile circuit at 104 mph to win the RAC Trophy.

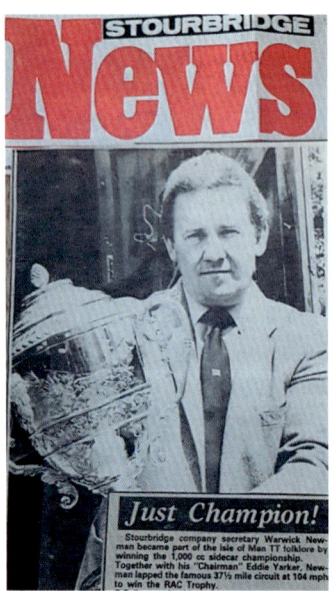

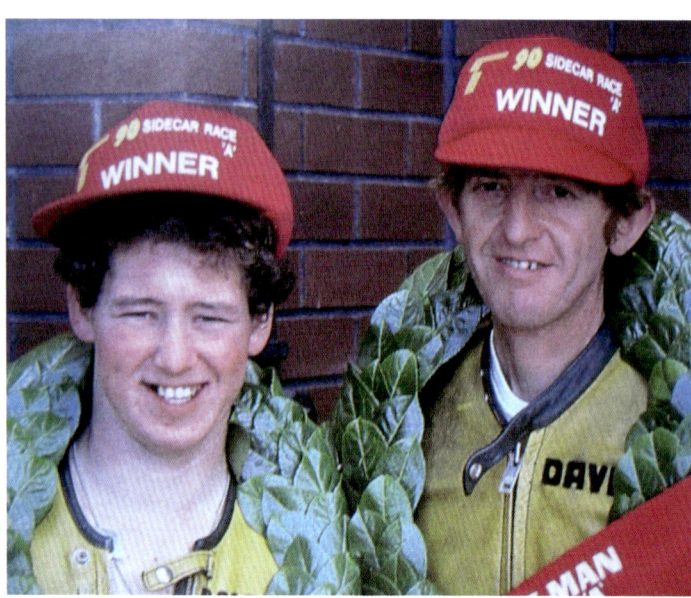

Mick Boddice and Dave Wells, after the 1994 Sidecar B TT. To their right sit winners Rob Fisher and Mick Wynn, and right of them, Dave Molyneux and Peter Hill. (Author's Collection)

Right: Dave Molyneux and Craig Hallam in practice for the 2006 TT. (Author's Collection)

Below: Dave Molyneux surveys the wreck of his outfit in his garage, following his 2006 practice crash. (Author's Collection)

Left: Dave Molyneux with the ACU Trophy, after winning the Bavaria sidecar Race B at the 2007 TT. (TT Press office)

Below: Five times TT winner Nick Crowe and passenger Mark Cox hold the ACU Trophy following victory in Race B at the 2008 TT. (Author's Collection)

Above: Klaus Klaffenböck and Dan Sayle following Klaffi's second TT win, 2010. (Courtesy of Isle of Man Newspapers)

Right: Tim Reeves and Dan Sayle following Reeves' first TT win, 2013. (Courtesy of Isle of Man Newspapers)

Above: Ben and Tom Birchall following victory in a European World Championship round. (Author's Collection)

Below: A rare look under the skin as Ben and Tom Birchall unload their lap record-shattering machine in 2018. (Author's Collection)

750 or 700 depending on what cylinders you used. But it was a lovely bike, very kind, very reliable. And George did the engine, I never touched the engine at all. We had one mechanic who came with us to do the chassis, which I was quite capable of doing, but they did it down south and so they were more familiar with it than I was, and I wasn't so much hands on at that particular time with the mechanic-ing for George because the bike was pretty much ready, I think it was everything else that wasn't ready, the bike was always done first![1]

O'Dell went to the 1977 TT in the midst of his campaign for the World Championship title that year. Although this was the first time that a TT win would carry no points towards that title, the two sidecar races on the Isle of Man were still eagerly anticipated, and certain to be hotly contested. The first practice session on the Island demonstrated just how severely an outfit could be battered by the bumpy roads – the Windle came back in to the pits with a main chassis tube broken, a loose rear sprocket, and a crack to a rear suspension mount. It took an all-night session in a rented garage in Douglas to put the damage right, but the outfit was ready for the second sidecar practice, run the following afternoon. O'Dell and the mechanics also made a series of modifications, including going up a jet size on the carburettor to 310 instead of 300 used on the UK circuits, in order to give more power on the climb up the Mountain. They had also used a harder spark plug, an N82G, in order to prevent it melting with the heat and possibly dropping into the cylinder, and opted to put a size 19 sprocket (the largest) on the engine with the smallest possible (a 33) on the rear wheel. When it was airborne, the engine would rev to an additional 1,000rpm before the back wheel bit into the road again, pulling the engine back with enormous force as it did so. All of that force was transferred through the chain, and at the Isle of Man TT a chain could stretch by as much as the length of a link over several laps. To help cope with this the chain manufacturer Renold had supplied O'Dell with a new experimental version made of harder steel, which reduced stretching considerably. There was nothing experimental or revolutionary about his tyres, however, they were standard Goodyear G50 slicks. His radiator was one from a cannibalised Suzuki road bike, fitted because it was considerably lighter than the Yamaha equivalent, and at a slight angle in order to minimise the damage caused by stones flicked out from the rear wheel of an outfit in front.

The magical 100mph sidecar lap had almost been achieved in 1976, when Mac Hobson and Mick Burns had lapped at 99.962mph. Now there was much speculation as to whether 1977 would see the barrier broken. With the bike back in good order and with his familiarity with the mountain circuit returning after a year away, O'Dell felt confident enough to push things as hard as he could during the second practice. After the first two laps O'Dell pulled into the pits to check that everything was still in place on the bike, and to make sure that his passenger Kenny Arthur was comfortable with the performance so far. On the third lap, from a standing start O'Dell launched the pairing into the history books, achieving an incredible 101.30mph. O'Dell remembered:

> It wasn't hard. There wasn't too much traffic out at the time, and any sidecars I did meet I seemed to catch at the best places to overtake without any trouble. There were a few corners that I went through very quickly, at a speed I didn't think a sidecar could go through. Quarry Bends we sailed through just like greased lightning. At Cronk Y Voddy and Sulby, I went through fairly gently because those straights are so bumpy. I got a bit of elevation at Ballaugh Bridge, which I normally do through failing to brake early enough. Over the Mountain I seemed to flash past the 32nd and 33rd milestones. Always have liked the Mountain section. But there were no problems at all. Didn't even get near any kerbs or grass.[2]

He continued with his description of the record-breaking circuit:

> Everything went so smoothly. I thought it was a good lap on the descent from the Mountain, coming down from Kate's Cottage to the Creg. The rest of the way home I knew there was only one place where there might be a hold up – Governor's Bridge. But there was only one bloke to pass after Governor's. Had we caught him going into Governor's he might have cost us 20 seconds which would have killed the lap. I'd watched Kenny out of the corner of my eye, flashing around, and I could tell he was enjoying himself. As I braked hard for Governor's the smell of burning brakes told me it must be a fast lap. I took it through the gears to 10,500 rpm as I screwed it

over the line. You can waste five seconds by rolling it off at the finish. I overshot the gate to the paddock and we had to wheel it backwards.[3]

For Kenny Arthur as well there was an instinctive feeling that this lap was 'the one'. He remembered:

It didn't feel a lot different or a lot harder, [but] it was obvious that the bike was very quick in a straight line, and at the Isle of Man that's quite critical, because you knew by the bumps and the bangs that you were getting going round various places [it] was a lot quicker than you had ever been before, so it was pretty obvious that we were very close; there and thereabouts for doing the 100 mile an hour. I'd been very close once before so I had a good idea what it was going to be like, and it was good, it was OK ... I felt very confident, I never felt in trouble with George at any state in my racing career ever, he would always seem to be in control, so I didn't have any qualms or questions, I just got on with the job ... When we got back we were quite shocked really. As soon as we rolled up in the paddock the boss of the Beresford [Hotel], John, he had a bottle of champagne, they were all standing there cheering and shouting, they said, 'You've done it, you've done it.' So, OK it was in practice, but it was done, and when we got back to the hotel they'd painted all the windows ... It felt really good, really special. You don't realise until later in your life how special that moment was, it's all in an adrenaline rush and 'of the moment'.

After the moment you realise what a part of TT history that was.[4]

A record lap in practice is always considered to be 'unofficial' but for O'Dell that day it made no difference. When the timing officials showed him the pink slip with his time noted on it he knew that he had achieved a personal ambition that he had been chasing since his crash at the TT in 1971. Since then, O'Dell's respect for the circuit had only increased but at the same time so had his determination to conquer it. At the time he learned of his achievement there were tears in his eyes, and that night he returned to the race office to stare at the practice leaderboard notice in the window, unable to take his eyes off his timing, before returning to the team lodgings at the Beresford Hotel where a party in his honour was in full swing.

For the first sidecar race of that 1977 TT O'Dell had been allocated the number sixteen, which greatly annoyed him. By rights he should have been in the top handful, but with a number as high as that he would have perhaps six crews to pass on the road before having a clear track in front of him, severely limiting his prospects in the race. His protests to the ACU fell on deaf ears, however, and there was nothing for it but for driver and passenger to equip themselves with a number of tear-off visors; there was a distinct possibility that they might get stuck behind another outfit blowing out oil mist and be unable to pass them for several miles. His chief opposition came in the form of Dick Greasley, with passenger Mick Skeels, and West German driver Rolf Steinhausen with passenger Wolfgang Kalauch. It was a four-lap race with a pit stop, and for the first two as predicted O'Dell encountered heavy traffic on the road, which caused him to lose concentration and also affected his speed. When he pitted, things got worse with first a jammed fuel filler nozzle and then fuel accidentally spilled all over the passenger platform that had to be cleaned up if Kenny Arthur was to have any chance of staying on board. The fuel was two-stroke mixture and Kenny remembered:

> It got a bit slippy, because there was oil in it and unfortunately we couldn't wipe it up. It was what they called a 'splash and dash' – it was a gallon in and then push off and you're ready to go. The other thing is, with a hot two-stroke engine, they really take a lot of pushing, and when you've just done two laps it's hard going. We pushed and pushed and then it fired up and we were gone, so it was good. It was a little bit slippy under foot, but I just managed to keep hold of the handles, I think that was important because it got on my leathers and on my knees, and with it having oil in the petrol I was sliding about a bit.[5]

However, even being told that Greasley had already lapped at over 100mph did not phase O'Dell; if anything it made him more determined, and on the next lap he settled into the job in hand. On the third lap he overhauled Steinhausen, and at Ballaugh a board told him he had a lead of two seconds over Greasley. By the final lap that was up to forty seconds and eventually, although he never managed to pass him or even catch him on the road, O'Dell took the race from Greasley by fifty seconds. In the process he had pushed up the sidecar lap record to 102.80mph. He remembered:

> The crowd made me do 102.80mph. As I was catching different guys, people could see me coming and would wave like mad at these other drivers, telling them to move over. It was incredible. During the last lap I was lapping the late starters and, at Ramsey, the crowd went wild as they urged two slower outfits to let me through. Talk about being switched on. The Island was being great to me and everything was going as smooth as silk. On the last lap ... I experienced one of my best feelings in racing. The spectators were urging me on, everyone seemed to be waving. At the Gooseneck where you're going slowly, you're almost in personal contact with the crowd who are just a few feet away. I could tell they were with me. They wanted me to catch Dick on the road – they knew he wasn't far ahead of me. Going through Brandish and Hillberry I thought some of them were going to get on my bike. They were going crazy and at Governor's I could hear them shouting.[6]

Everyone in the pits was elated, John Thompson from the Beresford Hotel had a Rolls-Royce waiting with champagne and took the team back to the hotel where more supporters were eager to greet the two and to congratulate them on their achievement. The Windle outfit was battered on its return to the pits – the engine was worn out and had to be replaced before the next race, and a number of cracks to the chassis had to be welded. Kenny Arthur too had taken a buffeting and had to visit an osteopath for treatment to his back before the second race. Even Greasley, who always felt that he had the better claim to be the one who achieved the first 100mph sidecar lap, had a grudging respect for O'Dell and his performance that day. Many years later he wrote on his website:

> In 1977 ... I had kicked off the season with a new Windle outfit with wider wheels for more rubber on the road (or grass ... delete accordingly!) and Mick Skeels took on the role of ballast. Although the chassis didn't handle as well as the previous sidecar, Mick and I got on well and immediately gelled putting in some solid performances. In our first TT together, there was great pressure as our main rivals had now also gone the 2 stroke route with Yamahas, Bartons or Konig adapted marine engines. I had also been given number 2, which meant I was the hare being hounded by those in my wake! From the onset, I gave all I could. Throughout practising I had been getting close to the 100mph lap, but I was surprised to achieve the first official ton sidecar lap on the mountain circuit and, certainly, from the standing start. George O'Dell has often been given the credit for it, but as he was following me, he wasn't the first over the line. But George was also flying that week and I have to say, he was exceptional in that race. His strength in some areas of the course were outstanding and he overtook me on the second lap and went on to win and complete the first ever 100mph average sidecar race.[7]

Race B was set to be another trailblazer and O'Dell was leading on time when the smell of burning clutch alerted him to possible problems. At Ballaugh the engine gave up the ghost, and he and Arthur spent the rest of the race in the Raven pub. O'Dell's main concern was that someone else would take his lap record, but he need not have worried. Even greater glory was to come for the Windle Yamaha later that year in the British Sidecar Grand Prix at Silverstone. O'Dell's other machine, a Seymaz, proved itself unreliable and so it was aboard his TT-winning outfit that he clinched the necessary points to secure the 1977 sidecar World Championship, the first British competitor to do so for twenty four years. Amazingly, O'Dell's championship came without him ever having won a race, so consistent was he in securing podium positions, and it was a strange irony that the only race that he did win that year – the Isle of Man TT – no longer counted towards a world title.

While the glory in 1977 belonged to O'Dell, second place in Race B that year went to another extraordinary character, who had only seen the course for the first time a few weeks earlier. His name was Rolf Biland, a Swiss sidecar racer and innovator. One of Biland's greatest attributes was self-confidence, and it is said that at that first visit to the TT that year he was taken on a tour of the Mountain circuit with other newcomers. While the others chatted among themselves, Biland sat in absolute silence, taking in everything he was seeing. Finally someone asked him what he thought of it all, and Biland broke his silence with a single sentence, 'I think I can win.'[8] At this time, several manufacturers were experimenting with a monocoque chassis; hub centre steering and car-type independent suspension were beginning to supplant traditional technologies in sidecar racing. Dick Hawes remembered that in 1977 he rode one such machine constructed by Formula 1 car chassis manufacturer British Racing Motors:

> Alex McFadzean and I rode the BRM in the first 4 lap race at the TT but the monocoque broke and the rear chain was the only thing holding it together. As we were on really good top start money (good old days) we made a start in the second race but had the van parked in the slip road at Braddan Bridge to collect us.[9]

He expanded:

> The outfit was financed by myself and was designed and constructed in the BRM workshop at Bourne in the winter of 1976–77. The motors used were Yamaha 500cc and 750cc four-cylinder. Initial testing was done at Donington on the 'test loop' over several Saturdays. George O'Dell was running the ex-Biland Seymaz at the time, which was of a similar configuration, and he was very helpful regarding setting up a 'short' wheelbase monocoque machine. The outfit was used in the 'four lap' TT race in 1977, where it finished despite not being suited to the bumpy circuit.[10]

Biland's other great strength was his willingness to think outside of the box, and he pushed developments being made by chassis manufacturers like Seymaz to their ultimate conclusion, as well as exploiting ambiguities in the sidecar racing rulebook.

Biland constructed a sidecar outfit under the name BEO, with a rear-mounted engine driving a single rear axle, which looked and handled more like a three-wheeled car – the outfit required no input whatsoever from the passenger, who simply sat in his seat for the whole race. It was an unsettling development for the sidecar racing community and threatened to break the sport's historic link to its roots in motorcycle racing. In 1980, the FIM responded by banning such prototypes, and the following year by bringing in new rules: there must be active participation from the passenger, the sidecar must be driven by a single rear wheel and steered by a single front wheel, and the driver must use motorcycle handlebars instead of a steering wheel. Biland, however, remains controversial for another reason, being one of those riders who walked away from the TT citing safety concerns, only to return later when start money improved.

The other Rolf who was closely associated with the sidecar TT at this time, Steinhausen, had no such qualms. The West German rider had stuck with König engines through the early 1970s and to be fair they had served him well. He had scored a first place in 1975 and 1976 but by 1978 he too was running Yamaha engines. HGV mechanic Steinhausen stated:

> If there were ten races in the Isle of Man at the same time as ten grands prix, I would go to the Island ... We finished third with a König [in 1973] when it was a world championship event but although I had to go on that occasion to get points I never regretted making the trip. I have been back every year since ... I just like going to the Isle of Man. I suppose you could say it is the

highlight of the year for me. The circuit is marvellous and I always get good treatment from the people in the Island themselves and the ACU. Since I had to go when it was a championship the ACU have always been very fair with me when it comes to money. [In 1973 a little] was all that I expected but since then it has got better every year ... We certainly do not go to the TT and stay at the Ritz. We are there to work, not play. It takes a long time to physically learn the course and you have to be able to give 100 per cent if you have any hope of putting in a winning speed ... I like to spend a lot of time working on the bike in the Isle of Man. It is a chance to get all the problems ironed out and I always think my machine is better for the TT visit ... I learned to strengthen certain parts because of the destruction that the Isle of Man circuit causes. There is no doubt that it is a hard circuit on machines but it is a public road not an ultra-smooth race track. Be prepared when it comes to machine preparation, that is my motto ... I feel a different rider when I get back from the Island. I find that I can ride faster in the grands prix. I feel to be living with my machine and they are not hard work any more.[11]

The first sidecar race of 1978 saw one of the blackest days in three-wheeled history on the Isle of Man. The race was only minutes old by the time three men lay dead; Mac Hobson and Kenny Birch died in a smash at the top of Bray Hill a few hundred yards from the start line. In a separate incident at the bottom of the hill Swiss rider Ernst Trachsel was killed after colliding with the debris, although his passenger escaped with a broken leg. The race went on, but such tragedy eclipsed the success of Biland in setting a new lap record before retiring shortly ahead of finishing. Hobson, from Gosforth, was a hugely popular character, and one of the biggest names in the North East Motorcycle Racing Club. He was in third place in the World Championships that year, and finished fifth posthumously. Knowing that Biland was faster, Hobson had planned to beat him to Quarter Bridge, but while overtaking had struck a raised manhole cover off the racing line. Tragically, the fact that there was a problem with this manhole cover following roadworks the previous winter was known, and it had been the subject of discussions between race organisers and representatives of the sidecar drivers the day before. The manhole was later removed, and 1978 was to be the last year that sidecars were set off from the line in pairs. The second race that year was taken by Steinhausen, with the up and coming talent of Mick Boddice in second place. Victory over the two legs went to another rising star, a young Scot named Jock Taylor.

John Robert 'Jock' Taylor was born in Pencaitland, near Edinburgh, and began racing in 1974 aged 19, as a sidecar passenger. By 1975 he was in the driving position, with an ex-Mac Hobson BSA twin. Like many other British champions he earned his spurs the hard way, struggling in his early club events with no financial backing. In those early years, he made do with worn tyres, tired engines and race fuel that was in short supply. One observer remembered that in his early days he would travel down to North Gloucester club meetings at Gaydon in Warwickshire. He used an old bus as a transporter and when it arrived at the trackside, out would pour a whole gang of faithful Scottish supporters. So loyal were these early fans that they even clubbed together to pay for the petrol to enable Taylor to get down to the meeting.

By 1977, Taylor had switched to Yamaha machinery and was starting to make a mark at British level, his most significant achievement up to that time being the setting of a new lap record of over 105mph at the Ulster Grand Prix. In the same year he won the Scottish Championship and came second in the British Championship with fellow Scot Lewis Ward in the chair. Together the two scored an eye-catching win at Oulton Park in Cheshire, and this brought Taylor to the attention of a major sponsor in the form of Fowlers of Bristol, one of the biggest motorcycle dealers in south-west England. In the 1978 season they backed him for a first attempt at the World Championship series. Despite Ward quitting midway through the year, with Fowlers' support Taylor put together a very creditable first season, with a third place in his home event, the British Grand Prix, fourth place in Czechoslovakia, sixth in Belgium, seventh in France and eighth in Italy, giving him an overall finish of seventh place.

The highlight of the 1978 season, however, was the Isle of Man TT, where with Kenny Arthur in the chair Jock Taylor finished second and third in the two sidecar legs, setting a new lap record of 101.22mph in the process. It was to be in 1979 that a winning pairing was born when, finding himself without a passenger for the Snetterton Race of Aces event, he appealed over the circuit public address for someone to come forward. From out of the solo paddock came a young Swede who had so far enjoyed only modest success – 22-year-old Bengt-Goran (Benga) Johansson. After completing his two years of national service in the Swedish army, Johansson (who was the son of a stock car racer from Ljungby near Anderstorp) rode a Morbidelli to second place in the Swedish championship, but struggled to break into the Grand Prix circuit and sold the machine. Having tried his luck at UK meetings he had again achieved only patchy success. His interest in sidecars was slight until that day when he answered Taylor's appeal, but the two clicked right away and became a pairing for the remainder of Taylor's career. With Johansson on board he took his maiden Grand Prix win just a few weeks after meeting him for the first time, appropriately enough in front of the passenger's home fans in Sweden. Up to that point, Taylor had been using a hub-centred Seymaz chassis, but later that year he acquired from Terry Windle a short-wheelbase outfit. It was on this machine that Taylor would enjoy so much success, both on and off the Isle of Man.

By 1980 the Scottish-Swedish pairing was poised for an all-out assault on the world title. Fowlers' racing boss, renowned engine builder Dennis Trollope, had put together no fewer than fifteen 500cc Yamaha engines on which to carry the world campaign, along with a further selection of 750cc motors for use in international meetings like the Isle of Man TT. With other financial backing in place as well, this meant that all Taylor had to supply was his riding talent. He took victory at the Dutch TT, and at the Grand Prix in Belgium and Finland, so that by the time he reached the British Grand Prix at Silverstone in August that year, the title was within his reach. Despite two of his main rivals dropping out with mechanical troubles, the race was still full of drama, with Taylor and Johansson suffering a slow puncture that cost them first place. Finishing second, however, was enough to hand them the 1980 world title. The same season had witnessed them raise the bar again at the TT, on the Windle chassis. Johansson had only seen the TT course for the first time in January of that year, and after an intense return visit in May in which he crammed in fifteen laps in a car, he felt that he knew the layout sufficiently well. In practice week his course knowledge grew further and he began to feel more and more comfortable with the Mountain circuit. His only difficulties, he recalled later, came from the bumpy surface (despite having fitted extra padding to the sidecar platform in order to try to compensate) and from the glare of the setting sun during evening practice sessions. After battling to second place in wet conditions during the first race, they won the Sidecar B event convincingly and chopped twenty-eight seconds off the lap record in the process, taking it now to 106.08mph.

In 1981 Taylor retained his British title and claimed further laurels in the TT, taking his tally of wins there to three. After wearing out two engines during practice week, they went into the first race with a brand new 700cc engine built just the night before by Dennis Trollope. Described by *Motorcycle News* as 'the world's most exciting sidecar partnership', the two set off at a blistering pace and took an astonishing 24.2 seconds off their record lap time from the previous year. Johansson added afterwards:

> Coming from the GPs, it was completely different. There was no scratching at all. It was damp in Ramsey so we had

to go carefully. I thought we'd do 103 or 105[mph]. I was really surprised we went round at 108mph.[12]

It was a close-run thing, however, as they finished the race with only fumes in the fuel tank, with Taylor explaining afterwards:

> We'd planned to stop for one or two gallons. But when it started to rain around Black Hut on the Mountain on the second lap I decided the extra petrol would be unnecessary.[13]

As the tail-enders completed their last lap, it developed into a real cloudburst but it was too late to really slow the leaders down. Among those tail-enders were newcomers Johnnie Rutherford and Barry Wallace, fellow Scots whose outfit number 78 was entered by T.B. Oliver Motorcycles of Hawick. Kawasaki powered, they used a largely standard engine for practice and a Moriwaki-tuned 'short circuit' engine for the race. One of their two mechanics kept a diary of their TT campaign in 1981, and described Race A:

> The starter's flag eventually dropped and Johnnie and Barry pushed off. The engine fired with no trouble and so they had started their first lap of the TT. Ian and I settled down in the pits surrounded by tools and spare wheels. They weren't needed. The race turned out as uneventfully as the practice (for no. 78 anyway), with Johnnie and Barry circulating like clockwork, all three laps being close to 27m 30s ... Jock Taylor, Derek Bayley and Mick Boddice

had all finished and were on the rostrum while Johnnie and Barry were still racing. I know it's not likely that they would put in a 10 minute lap, and so win, but they might at least have waited until everyone had finished!

In the finisher's enclosure there was much back-slapping and congratulations. Johnnie said that he felt much better than in practice, more relaxed and less tired. I got the impression that Barry knew the circuit much better now, and this helped Johnnie a lot. Apparently the race was just like the practice. Jock Taylor came past at Kirk Michael, but they saw very little of anyone else.[14]

The team had shared space in Douglas taxi-owner Jimmy Stoddart's large garage with three other crews, and it turned out that Rutherford and Wallace, who would have been pleased just to finish in this their first race, had done better than any of the others, coming thirty-third out of forty who finished. The machine, however, had received a severe battering from the bumpy course, much as it had in practice week:

We all felt quite pleased with ourselves. However, we came back to earth when, on checking the bike over, we found two more bad cracks on the frame and another leak in the petrol tank. So we resigned ourselves to completely stripping the bike yet again. Other than another oil and filter change, the engine, thank God, needed no attention.[15]

In the second sidecar event that year, the winners from Race A really showed how far ahead of the rest of the field they were.

In spite of mechanical problems, which meant their speed was considerably down on the first outing, they still beat second-place man Dick Greasley by nearly two minutes. They had started off slowly in order to try to preserve the Yamaha motor, and were hoping to complete the three laps without stopping for fuel. Only if they had been pressed seriously and forced to thrash the engine would they have to come into the pits. At first they were trailing main rival Trevor Ireson. However, after Ballaugh Bridge they were in the lead by five seconds, even though they had experienced a major slide at the thirteenth milestone, after which Taylor slackened off again. The real drama, however, began on the mountain climb on the second lap when the fuel pump gave out, and they had to hand pump petrol to the engine. Yet it was still a commanding victory.

It was 1982 that was to see Taylor and Johansson's greatest achievement at the Isle of Man TT, although it was a disappointing story in the first sidecar race when, despite being favourites, the duo hit big problems on the first lap. Taylor was distracted by the temperature gauge, and they clipped a bank. They eventually finished eighteenth, while Mick Boddice, who led for two laps, was forced to retire on the final lap with engine failure. Trevor Ireson (with passenger Donnie Williams) moved to the top of the leader board and had no such worries, taking the chequered flag in front of Greasley and Hanks.

Boddice's bad luck continued in the second race, which took place in glorious conditions. He led Taylor by a fraction of a second when he was forced out at Sulby Crossroads on the second lap. Taylor was cruising initially, as he needed to run in his Yamaha engine following an all-night repair job to fix a broken cylinder head stud, but turned up the wick to put himself four seconds ahead at the halfway point. With the departure of Boddice, Taylor took over control of the race, and even though he stopped for fuel at the end of lap two, he still managed to shave two seconds off his lap record from the previous year. In the final blistering circuit he increased the lap record to 108.29mph, to win from husband and wife team Dennis and Julia Bingham, and Steve Abbott with Shaun Smith in third. Overall victory from the two races went to Roy Hanks and Vince Biggs, who were fifth in that second race, but Taylor's lap record was an astonishing achievement. Some measure of this can be gained from the fact that it stood unbroken for seven years. Indeed, there were some who said it would never be broken, and as the years rolled on, changes to the course (particularly to smooth out Sulby Straight, which at that time was like riding on corrugated iron, and to Quarry Bends, which after road alterations became a gear faster) meant that it never could be beaten. Taylor himself put his astonishing speed down to the fact that this time round he had moved the temperature gauge, so that it was now Johansson's responsibility to watch it!

Just weeks after their achievement in the TT, Taylor and Johansson travelled to take part in the Finnish Grand Prix. Taylor had been developing a long-wheelbase machine to compete in World Championships, and although he did not like the outfit due to its unfortunate tendency to leap across the road, he had decided to persevere with it. The more reliable four times TT-winning short-wheelbase machine was left at home, prepared in readiness for the forthcoming British Championship round at Donington. On race day at the Finnish circuit at Imatra, like the TT also a closed roads course, the heavens opened. Jock was the sidecar riders' representative and gave the go ahead for the sidecar Grand Prix to take place. It was a decision to have fateful consequences. In the rain-soaked conditions, Taylor and Johansson's outfit aquaplaned and slid off at a corner, colliding with a telegraph pole as it did so. Taylor survived the initial impact, but as he was receiving attention from marshals at the scene another machine (piloted by a Finnish rider) suffered a similar misfortune and slid off at the same place. It collided with the wreckage of Taylor's outfit and the race was red flagged as medics attended the injured. He died that evening from the injuries sustained in the second crash. For his family and friends, the news was made all the more shocking by the fact that they learned of Jock's death via a BBC sport broadcast that night. Even today, more than thirty years after his death, many TT fans and competitors alike regard Jock Taylor as the greatest ever sidecar racer.

In 1983, there was the only TT appearance of Steve Webster, ironically arguably Britain's most successful sidecar racer with an incredible tally of ten World Championships and an MBE to his name. Webbo to his friends, he followed in the footsteps of his father Mick Webster, who raced Triumph-powered outfits in the 1960s and 1970s. Steve was an apprentice at Rowntree Mackintosh chocolate in York when he took up racing. Eventually he was asking for so much time off to go to meetings that the firm gave him an ultimatum – either give it up or take redundancy. Webster chose the latter and got into sidecars full time. However, he made less than half a lap in his first race on the Isle of Man before disaster struck at the thirteenth milestone:

> I still can't remember anything about it really; I must've got the 13th wrong! I ended up in Nobles hospital with compressions of the neck. My passenger, Tony Hewitt, broke a couple of vertebrae.[16]

Also in 1983, after years as the TT bridesmaid with his efforts constantly thwarted by mechanical failures, Mick Boddice scored his first win in Race B of that year, with regular passenger Chas Birks. Having broken his duck, there was no holding Boddice back and he would go on to win a further eight races in the 1980s and into the 1990s. He picked up sponsorship along the way from Suzuki spares dealer Bran Bardsley, while the Woodhouse brothers provided his chassis. Meanwhile, fellow Birmingham racer Roy Hanks recalled:

> Though everyone was chuffed to bits with us winning overall in 1982, in 1983 I tried to win a race outright. We were now running Z700s that were even quicker than the 750s. The 700 was the older version but as it didn't have those read valves the carburation was better. We came third but I came back having scared myself to death, as I just knew I wasn't in control. This thing was like, aim-and-go-and-brake, and they were talking about speeds of 180mph coming down off the Mountain. That's daft.[17]

Although Ireland has supplied numerous riders who have enjoyed solo success at the TT, sidecar drivers and passengers from the shores of Erin have been notably less conspicuous. One exception was Alan Langton, who first raced on the Island in 1983:

I was just 21 and had gained my International Passenger Licence, went to the TT as a freelance passenger and got a run with Tony Barker, who was the current European champion. The lap record at the time was 108mph and we did the elusive 100mph lap on our first lap of race one and we were lying sixth. Unfortunately we retired on lap two, and in the second race we retired on the third lap, which was a little frustrating. '84 was another disaster of a year with Steve Sinnott and we didn't finish a race, but for '85 I partnered Lowry Burton, and while we retired in race one we finished second in race two, which was brilliant.[18]

In fact, Lowry Burton is regarded by many as Ireland's greatest ever sidecar competitor. Starting out on Irish circuits in the 1970s, he secured the Irish Championship in 1978 with Marty Murphy. The duo retained the title in 1979 and also made their debut at the TT. In 1980, Burton became friends with Jock Taylor, and with Pat Cushnahan in the chair scored wins in 1986 and 1987. Burton's proudest achievement, however, was to twice win the Jock Taylor Trophy for the fastest lap. In his opinion Jock was the greatest ever TT sidecar racer. With no three-wheeled racing on the roads north or south of the border now, it is difficult at present to envisage Ireland ever producing another sidecar TT winner.

In 1984, future World Champion Steve Abbott finally clinched a TT win in Race 2, after four years of trying. Husband and wife team Dennis and Julia Bingham's outfit broke down in the same race when their gearbox failed, robbing them of potentially winning the sidecar championship. The Binghams' outfit was built by Terry Windle specifically for the conditions found at the TT; there was more ground clearance than for short-circuit events, and to make sure the Padgetts-sponsored outfit would endure three laps of the bumpy Mountain Course at race speeds, Windle had used heavier-gauge tubing at vital points on the chassis for extra strength. After seven years of TT racing and three runner-up positions, the duo were hoping for better things in 1985. Indeed, Julia had hopes of being the first female winner of a TT, commenting:

> I didn't use to think about it at all, but now after standing in the second place spot on the rostrum three times I am thinking 'let's get to the number one place'. Yes it would be nice to leave my name somewhere in the record books … I was very disappointed last year, I admit, because I thought that if we had made second place in the second race, we would have been the overall winners. To do that would have been an added bonus. Although there is no extra money it is the achievement of finishing well up in both races that counts. Well there's no overall winner this year, we'll just have to win the races outright.[19]

Her husband Dennis added:

> Like all new machines it had a few teething troubles to iron out and I was surprised that we did so well [last year]. This year the outfit is proven. We have a similar 700cc engine to last year and providing everything stays together I feel we have the ability to win … The important thing

about the TT is adopting an entirely different approach to machine preparation. Every nut and bolt has to be wire locked, and we do things like fitting two batteries and two fuel pumps to make sure we get home. You never seem to be out of the garage, especially during practice week. You go to practice, return to the garage and spend hours of work on the machine. The work ends just before it's time to go out on the Course again.[20]

The Binghams felt they had the crucial element of teamwork between passenger and driver, and Julia contended:

I can tell by the way Dennis is moving about on the outfit just what he's going to do. I think at times I know what action he's going to take before he does himself ... The Island is certainly not the place to have a new passenger jump into the chair. It's essential on the track to be able to put complete trust in each other.[21]

Giving the example of 1984 winners Steve Abbott and Shaun Smith, she added:

When Shaun was out of action a couple of years ago through injury, Steve was never happy, you could tell.[22]

Despite their preparations, 1985 was not to be the Binghams' year, although they would go on to achieve another second place in 1987. That same year nephew Tom Hanks joined veteran Roy as passenger. There was a lot to learn as a newcomer and, as

Tom remembered, it was amazing how many armchair experts there were. Everyone he spoke to had an opinion on this corner or that corner, and the best way to take it. It would not have been so bad if the 'experts' could agree. After introduction to the delights of early morning practice, Race Day came around. Race 1 resulted in a DNF. Then came Race 2:

> Before the race I was sure we wouldn't finish, too many things had gone wrong during practice. Waiting for our 5 second call was the worst bit. I thought the lights had broken down, or the fellow with the flag had fallen asleep, it seemed to drag on forever. When the flag finally fell for us, I was breathless. I couldn't even push the bike, I was gasping for air through holding my breath waiting for the flag.
>
> Then we were away and flying, it felt much better than practice. I remember not getting up for the left-hander at Union Mills and thinking that the crowd looked a bit surprised, not half as surprised as Roy though. Apart from passengering I was supposed to turn the petrol taps on and off. I was meant to do this when Roy gave the 'pre-planned signal.'
>
> However, while we were going up the mountain mile and I was busy hanging out for the fast left hander, that never arrived, Roy gave me a signal to keep down, which co-incidentally was identical to the turn the tap off signal. This really threw me so [I] just left the tap alone and worried about it for the rest of the race.
>
> A mate was keeping us informed with signals on how we were doing and I really started to enjoy myself

when I saw we were doing OK ... I then waved at some Germans that were waving at us on the mountain. The last time through Governor's Bridge I thought this is it, we're going to finish.[23]

In 1988, there was a double win for Mick Boddice, while for Roy and Tom Hanks, Race A of that year almost ended in utter disaster. Roy, however, was honest about the cause:

I crashed because I was treating the TT Course with contempt: I'd been coming for a long time even then. I'd caught up with the eventual winner and there were three outfits in front of me coming into the 33rd. I could have passed one of them coming into the 33rd, and all of a sudden I was thinking about glory and about how good it would look out-braking the lot of them on the run down to Creg ny Baa. Suddenly they all turned left-and I didn't! I should have been concentrating on what I was doing, but I was getting ahead of myself, already at the Creg thinking about how good it would look on camera. And that was it, we crashed.

If something goes wrong in a sidecar, you get up and hit the passenger even if it's not his fault, because then at least the crowd think it was his fault! But I'd shot Tom so far off down the side of the mountain (he'd broken his femur) and I had two broken ankles, and all I could think about was getting the bike ready for Monday's race! Since then a lot of people have said that the wind caught us and blew us off the road, others have said I was using the wrong tyres, but I have to say now, hand on heart, if I'd have been concentrating on what I was doing we wouldn't have crashed.[24]

In 1989, Boddice won Race 2 at 107.17mph, pipping by a couple of seconds Jock Taylor's lap record, which everyone had thought would stand forever, whilst Manx driver Dave Molyneux scored his maiden win aboard the Bregazzi Yamaha in Race 1. As the son of 1970s sidecar passenger John Molyneux, sidecars were in Dave's blood and he began racing as soon as he was able to, aged 16. He drew his inspiration both from his father and his boyhood hero, George O'Dell, who he watched in action at the 1977 TT. Initially his mother had to sign his competition licences, but as Dave recalled later, if she had refused he would just have forged her signature and gone racing anyway. Eric Bregazzi, an old friend of John's, had given Dave his outfit when he retired and together with his father Dick Bregazzi, was his first main sponsor and helper. During these years Eric could never understand why the outfit kept breaking gearbox cogs. Dave professed not to know either, and didn't tell him that in his pursuit of extra speed he just didn't bother with the clutch and crashed the gears every time he changed up or down. He remembered:

> It was a strange race, because we got set off on our wrong start time. There was somebody in front of us who missed his start position, and that set the grid off in the wrong sequence. So I got to the end of the race, and I thought we'd finished second, losing out by a couple of seconds.

But I was pretty happy with that because it was a hard race, and the bike didn't run exceptionally well, it could have run better. Two strokes are very fickle, and on that particular day it could have run a lot better. When you get to the bottom of Bray Hill, you usually know if the bike is going any good, and on this occasion it just didn't feel that great; but we just accepted that, it was our fault because we'd set it up. But we got to the Park Ferme afterwards well happy at the thought we'd finished second, and then somebody, I think it was Geoff Cannell the roaming commentator, came and said, 'Something's wrong here, Dave has won it, he ain't second.' There was a lot of confusion, but then it was announced over the Tannoy that we'd actually won the race on corrected time, because there had been this cock-up on the start line. So it was official that we'd actually won the race! It was a roller coaster of emotions for me. Deep down I was a little disappointed in the fact that the bike had not gone as well as it had done in practice, and with such a small margin of losing out, I thought, you know if it had been right we could have walked that race, but then at the same time I figured, 'What the hell, we're second, it's my first podium position ever, so that'll do for today. We'll have better luck next time …' And the next thing I know, I've won it! Luckily this was all sorted out in the Park Ferme, before we went up onto the rostrum, so we went up there as winners! We got the champagne, and the winners' laurels on our first time up there.[25]

Part of the reason for Molyneux's success was the fact that he had decided to redesign the bodywork of his Ireson chassis machine along his own lines, and ended up with a far more streamlined and efficient profile as a result. It was the first step towards becoming not just a rider, but a sidecar constructor.

However, things were evolving at the TT and this would be the last year of the big 1,000cc Yamaha engines. In the 1990 season, the TT changed massively for sidecars, with the event going to Formula Two class. The change was prompted by the generally poor state of sidecars at that time. Outfits were being built for 500 and 750cc two-stroke engines, which were tiny motors. They were quite lightweight, and initially intended for Grand Prix use. Riders were then buying those bikes second-hand, and adapting them to fit a cost-effective engine to go TT racing with. This would usually be a 1,000cc Suzuki, Kawasaki, or Honda; big four-strokes that were nearly double the weight of the engine that the chassis was originally designed to carry. As a result accidents were happening with increasing frequency; frames were breaking, and racers were losing their lives because the general state of the outfits was dreadful. In the end the ACU had to do something. The machines at the TT weren't getting any faster, they were just getting more dangerous. So the organisers thought that if they changed the rules, people would have to build new bikes, and build them suited to the engines they are actually going to use. The specification for TT sidecars was reduced from 1,000cc down to Formula Two regulations, which was 350cc. Competitors could also ride a 600cc four-stroke in Formula Two as they can today, but those engines were so old fashioned and heavy in those days that they simply were not competitive against a 350cc two-stroke Yamaha.

Many riders were against this change at the time. To them it bordered on the ridiculous to change from a 1,000cc limit to a 350cc limit. Then the ACU also brought in the four-stroke 600cc class, which was not even filtered into the event, it was simply announced that it was happening. It became a superb class, and looking back the organisers made the correct decision to bring that in. But the ACU got this right by sheer luck, rather than by judgment, because it took a long time for the 600cc engines to develop into a great racing class. Back in 1990, 600cc four-strokes were not even a great solo class, because not all the manufacturers even produced a decent engine for racing at that size back then. The ACU brought that class in to placate people who did not like the fact that all their hard work and all the sponsorship they had raised – tens of thousands of pounds worth to finance the 750cc two-stroke Yamahas that many were running – had just been wasted. Other people were running 1,000cc Suzukis or Kawasakis, and these bikes also became obsolete in terms of the TT overnight. They were now just scrap – they had a TT-winning bike one day, and then the next they had a bike that didn't suit the TT or anywhere else.

From 1984 to 1989 the sidecar TT had included Formula 2 races with the overall field. The Formula 2 subclass had been largely dominated by Dave Saville in these years, so it was no surprise that in 1990, the first year of universal Formula 2 regulations across the board, Saville with passenger Nick Roche took victory in both sidecar TT races in his Sabre Tools-sponsored machine, posting a lap of 100.97mph in the process. Saville, an engineer from Ranskill, near Retford in Nottinghamshire, was well aware of the limitations of a Formula 2 outfit on the TT course but at the same time had the experience to work around them, having competed at the event since 1968. He noted:

> The smaller machine tends to jump about a bit going down Bray Hill because being so much lighter it tends to pick up the bumps ... With the 350 it's a matter of grin and bear it while the [outfit] picks up speed on the climb towards Glen Vine. [Through Crosby and up to Greeba] it's not easy, Boddice dropped Chas Birks there for example and even the 350 gets its back out and drifts on the right-hand exit ... It's so important not to catch another outfit on the climb up to Sarah's Cottage because if you have to back off it costs seconds, and seconds more going on to the Cronk Y Voddy straight ... A 350 leaps a bit and if you hit the bottom [of Barregarrow] with a thud it can stretch the chain or crack a frame tube. It's the same at Ballaugh, which I aim to trickle over and then turn on the power ... I never go to the right side [at Milntown] because the bumps pull you further to the right side of the road. Coming up the middle of the road may seem like the wrong line but it does not matter because you have to shut off for the bumps and there is the right side to play with in case of emergency.

It is bumps again which make Cruickshanks one of the slowest parts of the Course for an F2 outfit and although I change up to go through Stella Maris, everything is dying off because of the start of the climb to the Hairpin, which is best dealt with by a steady approach and a power-on exit. Coming out of Waterworks and through the series of rights and lefts up to the Gooseneck, the front end of my outfit is jumping all over the place. Fortunately the surface smooths out on the braking point for the right-hander so it's possible to get the power turned on for the long climb that takes everything out of a 350. It depends on the wind whether to stay in fifth or hit top for Guthries, and I am still waiting for the revs to build up.[26]

Saville credited passenger Nick Roche with helping him to perfect the approach to Hillberry, adding:

I always used all the road, which did not please me too much, but when I mentioned it to him after a practice session he told me to let him sort it out. He did just that and since then I always come out in the middle of the road for the approach to Cronk ny Mona, where I drop to fifth to keep the revs buzzing.[27]

His 1990 victories placed him within one win of becoming the most successful sidecar racer in TT history, and Saville opted to stick with his 350cc two-stroke for 1991 simply because it was the devil he knew. He commented at the time:

My whole season revolves around getting into double figures and being the TT top man. I am desperate to win and I suppose that is putting me under more pressure this year than I have been in the Island for a long time ... At one stage I was planning to switch to a 600 four-stroke Yamaha this year but although Mitsui were prepared to supply the engines ... I have not raced a four-stroke for ten years so I would have been spending practice re-adjusting and that's not a good thing with so much at stake ... If they can get the bigger-capacity four-strokes running well there are places such as the Mountain climb where they will have a considerable power advantage over the 350s.[28]

In particular, he was aware of the threat presented by Mick Boddice:

Providing the Honda is running better than it was last year, and I am sure it will be, he could well make ten seconds each lap on me on that climb. Progress on the 350 is governed dramatically by the prevailing weather conditions and if there is a lot of wind in the right direction it is possible to pull top at the Mountain Box providing it is possible to keep the engine revs up.[29]

Saville and his ageing 350cc two-stroke certainly gave the opposition a run for their money. Dave Molyneux and Karl Ellison put the lap record up from 102 to 104mph that year on their Kawasaki-powered machine, while Saville was lapping at around 102mph, so was only a fraction behind. But the fact of the matter was that he had got the absolute maximum out of his engine, and it was becoming obvious by then that the

350cc two-stroke was never going to be competitive at that level again. Now, the new generation of 600cc four-strokes that were coming along had shown themselves to be far superior.

As evidence of how far and how fast the four-strokes had come on by 1991, Mick Boddice had won both races that year on a 600cc Honda; he had now got major factory support for the first time in his career, but initially at least this was not of the level that he might have hoped. Honda offered him an engine, but as Mick recalled:

> We were sent round the back streets to a place where they kept the test fleet and there was our bike at the back. It was an ex-press test bike, 90,000 miles on the clock and thrashed by everyone who'd sat on it. They were surprised I finished second on it [in 1990] and I was 10 years with them after, when I'd get two engines a year.[30]

In 1992 Geoff Bell, whose brother Ian ran a Yamaha dealership in Newcastle, also achieved a double win on a 600cc engine from that manufacturer. In the solo classes the 600cc engine had really come on as well, indeed it was the basis of the later Supersport 600cc engines. The Yamahas were very fast and extremely powerful, so it was becoming obvious now which was the best motor to use in a sidecar application; this engine dominated sidecars for the next five or six years, more so than any other type of motor.

Ironically, Mick Boddice's decision to become a Honda-supported driver might actually have cost him races. The 600cc Honda was a good engine, but it was a harder job to make it a fast engine than it was with the Yamaha equivalent. It was that bit more difficult, so for most people involved in racing the Yamaha was the more favoured motor to use. Engine tuners did not really have to do a lot to it, it was fast straight away, whereas they had to do more work to the Honda to make it a quick engine for a sidecar, and it was naturally more expensive to do that as well. Boddice was widely regarded as a brilliant driver, and this combined with the fact that he had highly skilled people working on his engines made him competitive. Throughout the 1993 season and into 1994 he was a particularly hard man to beat on the track, but this competitive edge did not last.

The Yamahas came on a lot faster, as did the drivers who were using them. There were soon more Yamahas on the grid than any other make. Another advantage lay in the fact that they were also smaller engines. They were compact and they suited the chassis better, and also they were lower. From 1993 onwards, the Yamaha 600cc power unit was *the* engine to use at the TT – certainly at the sharp end of the grid anyway. There were unexpected consequences of this – things became a lot more competitive in the sidecar paddock for one thing. In the old days, anyone would have lent a competitor a crank. From 1993 onward it was still possible to borrow bits from other competitors but it was not so easy – there was a lot more rivalry. Another unintended consequence was that although Formula 2 rules had been introduced to try to lower the overall cost of the sport, and make it more affordable, it did not work because it cost a lot more to make those modern four-stroke engines competitive. Dave Molyneux took his first double victory in 1993 on Yamaha power. He remembered:

In 1993 it all just came together, all that being patient and not so bloody headstrong started to pay off. The first bike that I built which I put a real big effort into, and which needed money behind it, was the one I used in the 1993 TT. I put together what I really wanted to put together. It was my own design, which drew on elements of all the other bikes I had ever ridden, and there was a few grand chucked in the pot as well, from various local sponsors. It worked – it might have been a lucky design, I don't know, though I feel that it was judged well – but it really worked, and all my outfits up to now have been based on that bike. I didn't work from blueprints, it was all in my head, I just started with some steel tubing, and we got what turned out to be the best engine of that time in it, the 600cc Yamaha. By that time, having proved also that I could construct something that was safe, new parts started coming through from suppliers. That year, 1993 we cleaned up. The TT was ours for the taking. We were the quickest in practice and had the fastest lap in both races, lap records, race records, won the double, and it came easy. It all just fell together. It was an outstanding package that we put together that year, but I don't just mean the bike when I say that, I include Karl Ellison in there as well. He was probably the best available passenger at that time – he was possibly one of the best in the world back then in fact – he was very good at it, and not only that he's also a clever man, who's got a very good head on his shoulders; he was particularly good at analysing things and talking things through after a race, which not every passenger is.

> I only finished building the bike in the week running into the event. We did Jurby road circuit on the Saturday and won that, then we went out on Monday morning practice for the TT and were quickest instantly. It was all plain sailing with that bike. We literally strolled it. The first race we had a race record and a lap record. The second race again it was a stroll. It really was a very easy win. When I say it was easy, I mean that it didn't feel that fast after we had been riding Formula One machines a few years earlier. It's important to remember that those early Formula Two bikes were very slow compared to what we see now. They didn't accelerate like they do now, didn't corner like they do now, and they didn't have the top speed. But we were really delighted with that result, it was a major achievement; a double win for a start, but also I'd done it on my own bike, and from then on everybody wanted one. It was a turning point for me, as then I really got my teeth into building my own bikes and that's what got me race wins. I'm a good rider, but I'm not brilliant by any stretch of the imagination. However I'm as good at building bikes as I am at riding, and together that's a successful combination.[31]

In 1993 came the arrival at the TT of Rob Fisher. The West Cumbrian motorcycle mechanic was an experienced British Championship driver and had taken the title in 1991 and 1992. He got into the TT almost by accident – a suitable Formula 2 machine came his way via a sponsor and he thought the TT might offer valuable experience. He learned the course via on board videos and his appearance in 1993 was intended to be a one-off, but so good was his performance that he scored a top six position in Race A and probably would have achieved something similar in Race B were it not for a broken fuel pump. This led to his decision to make a comeback in 1994, and using only a stock FZR600 engine acquired from a breaker's yard he sensationally won both races. Fisher's double win further underlined the dominance of the Yamaha power unit in the mid-1990s. He remembered:

> The second year we had much more time to prepare … When [passenger] Mick Wynn got on board with us I was starting to get a bit of a team together, plus Mick had already done the TT so he knew his way around. It just all fell into place really.[32]

Wynn had ridden with Craig Hallam as driver in the early 1990s, and now noticed an immediate difference in power, with Fisher's four-stroke accelerating dramatically. Even so, 1994 was not without drama, as he added later:

> We had blown our race engine in practice, so there was a certain amount of finger-crossing that we'd last the distance. In truth, we were strong from the off and never looked back.[33]

Fisher's great strength was that he understood the psychology of racing, the mind games that could unsettle an opponent, and the fact that all out speed in a straight line wasn't everything.

Sometimes if you kept the pressure on, you could force a rival to make a mistake. In 1995 he was also on form. However, a crash in practice, when he slid into a wall, left the machine mangled. In stepped arch-rival Dave Molyneux (who was having bike issues of his own to contend with that year) to fix the damaged chassis. Fisher repeated his feat from the previous year, with a new race record in Sidecar A, together with a lap record, and in Sidecar B again the race record was broken. Of the latter, Molyneux remembered:

> We were ready and we went out for the second race, and that was a saga all in itself. We were in the warming up area, all full of confidence and fired up to Hell. We were going to get one back on Rob, or so we thought. We started the bike, and it only ran on three cylinders. I thought, 'Christ what's going on here,' so in a panic, because there was only five minutes to go to the start of the race, we took the seat off, replaced all the spark plugs and it ran on all four cylinders again. We thought, 'Great!' We put the seat back on, and pushed the machine up to the start line. The three-minute board came up, and I sat on the bike. As I did so the kneeling tray on the right-hand side of the seat sank down. I looked under it, and saw that it hadn't gone back into its locating peg when we had put the seat back. My brother by this time had gone off to the pit area, and I didn't have a screwdriver to get the seat off. So I lay under the bike, and I had to use both my thumbs to lever the carbon-Kevlar bodywork over the peg. As I did so, I dislocated my left thumb! It was literally bent back

touching my wrist! I yelled out, 'AAAGH!!! F***ING HELL!!!' We were there on the start line, about to race, and the two-minute board now came up. Peter Hill pulled my glove off, and there was a blue crease around the base of my thumb where it was dislocated. He said to me, 'Dave, you can't ride like that!!' I yelled back, 'I can!!' I put my hands between my legs, yanked my thumb and felt it go back into its socket, put my glove straight back on and off I went for the start of the race! It happened literally that fast! I thought to myself, 'This is just a f***ing *disaster*!! Everything is against us this year. This is just not meant to be!' So I had all these stupid thoughts in my head, wondering if I should carry on, and worrying for most of the first lap that if the handlebars got into a wobble it would push my thumb back out of its socket. We carried on, but the front brake master cylinder failed, which supplied the front discs, so we then only had a back brake and sidecar wheel brake. That was halfway round and we nearly went straight on at Ramsey Hairpin as a result, but still we finished second. It was a good second, a strong second, but I thought, 'Thank Christ that's all over.' We had had a heavy week, a hell of a week in fact, but after it was all over Rob thanked me for fixing his bike!! I was glad that he won though, because I'd built a bike for someone who had gone on to win the TT with it – twice.[34]

After the 1995 TT Molyneux spent some time on the European circuits. It was in 1996, however, that he and passenger Peter Hill took the sidecar event at the Isle of Man TT to a whole new level. The machine that he was using was an improvement on any that he had ridden before at the TT, by a considerable degree. The bike had previously had a Krauser engine in, with which he had taken on the European meetings the previous year; since returning home he had cut the chassis in half, and put a whole new front on it to accommodate a 600cc Yamaha engine. It was also better than anything else partly due to the fact that Molyneux ran wider wheels in the European championship races, and he left those on it for the TT. The accepted thinking in those days was that narrower wheels were better for the Isle of Man roads. As usual, money played a big part in the decision-making process. Molyneux did not have the funds to change the wheels so in the end thought the cheaper option was just to get bigger tyres. So he went up from an 8in- to 10in-wide back wheel and discovered that it dramatically improved the steering. By sheer accident he had found a good formula between the wheels and his modified chassis. Also, the updated FZR600 motor, which was a newer-generation engine, was a lot better than that he had used before. It had nothing trick on it. It was a standard CDI ignition pack, which only revved to 12,000rpm as opposed to a modern 17,000rpm unit. It was carburettored, and did not have an air box on it. It was in many ways very basic, but Molyneux also had another secret weapon in the form of engine tuner Tony 'Slick' Bass, who did a truly impressive job on the engine, and the combination of that and the chassis he had put together sent it into another world.

It was ironic that the ACU had decided to get rid of the big-engined bikes at the TT because they were too fast and too dangerous. In doing so they changed to Formula 2 specification, and succeeded at first in reducing the speeds dramatically, by 7 or 8 miles an hour instantly, but then when they let the 600cc four-strokes in the speeds escalated so fast that by 1996 they were back up to and beyond those that had concerned them so much in the first place. Molyneux sums up what happened next:

> Then the 1996 Isle of Man TT came around, and we cleaned up. We absolutely bloody buried it. We knocked the record book for six. We had Slick Bass helping us that year. Slick was Carl Fogarty's crew chief in the four World Championships which he won, but he had just lost his job with Honda that year and was now back home in Ramsey. I asked him if he would tune our engine for the TT. He came down and helped us out, and did a great job. The existing lap record for Formula Two machines at the TT was 107 miles an hour in Rob Fisher's name, and the Formula One lap record was 108 miles an hour in Mick Boddice's name, and we lapped at 110 miles an hour on the first night of practice! The thing was we hadn't even ridden that bike on a circuit before. Before the TT we took it up the Jurby airfield straight, and I think it was on the third run up and down the straight that I decided the bike was probably as good as it was ever going to be. I came back in after that run and told my brother, 'I think we can go one tooth bigger on the gearing at the back, and that will do it. Other than that the bike feels pretty good.' Peter Hill agreed, and that was really all the preparation work we did on that bike. On the first night of TT practice, the Monday night, we did a 107

mile an hour lap from a standing start and 110 miles an hour on the second lap. We just blew the paddock apart. They couldn't believe it. Talk about moving the goalposts, that sent them into another age. I came in, and I knew it was good but I didn't know just how good. Actually it was quite hard for me to judge. I hadn't ridden a short-wheelbase bike for some time, and I was more used to the speeds on European Championship bikes.[35]

When they came in after that first practice, it was clear that passenger Peter Hill had had a rough ride. In fact, he told Molyneux that it was the worst ride he had ever had on the Isle of Man. What the speed was he did not know, but in his words it had nearly shaken him to bits. The back suspension on the outfit was untried as they had no run-up to the event, and no time to test it, so it was rather too solid and too stiff on the back, and this had contributed to Hill getting a severe shaking. His gums were bleeding; his chin was cut where he had caught it on the passenger handles keeping his head down out of the wind. It had also taken all the skin off his shins. However, like most passengers he was made of tough stuff, indeed Molyneux remembered him as one of the best in the business. He was a 'not-give-in' kind of man. He would never hit a driver on the back and cause him to stop, for any reason. After practice that night he was quite angry, but the mood quickly changed when at that point Molyneux's brother came running over to them with a stopwatch. Excitedly he told them that they had just done over 110mph. There was an air of disbelief at first, but he was adamant about the speed that had been achieved. For his part, Peter Hill's reaction was deadpan. He turned round to the Molyneux brothers without blinking and said: 'Well no f***king wonder my shins are bleeding!'[36]

It was a different story when they pushed the bike back down to the paddock; it was rather like someone had died, and the atmosphere was very sombre. The rest of the paddock were stony faced, and the rumours had already started. There was no celebration, and Molyneux simply put the bike in the van and went home. With only one good engine, they did just four laps of practice that week. But at the Grandstand during the next practice session, during scrutineering a fuel sample was requested, which was unusual. Clearly, there were suspicions that Molyneux and Hill were breaking the rules. Whispers were going around in the paddock, asserting that they had a big-bore engine in the outfit, that it was impossible for a Formula Two bike to go that fast, and that the only explanation was that they had to be cheating.

The allegations were somewhat illogical because even if they had been cheating and had a big-bore engine in, then they had still broken the record for that class by over 2mph, which would have been an even more unlikely achievement. In those days, in scrutineering the top of the engine had to come off. The scrutineers would then measure the cylinder bore and stroke, measure the size of the carburettor, and they would test the fuel. When Molyneux had been asked for the fuel sample on the Tuesday night of Practice Week, he had assured the scrutineers that it was simply premium unleaded and it had come from Kirk Michael filling station. It is important to remember that just prior to that, the ACU had banned leaded race fuel. In the years previously machines had been running on fully leaded, 118 octane high-performance race fuel, which was dangerous if it was not handled carefully, and expensive as well. When it was banned, it took a few years before high-octane unleaded race fuel became available, so for the time being teams had to use fuel from a roadside pump. Furthermore, no garage actually sold super unleaded on the Isle of Man at that point, so the fuel that they were using was the most basic type that could be found in any road-going vehicle around at the time. It was little wonder that the scrutineers were somewhat sheepish when tests proved this indeed to be the case.

Molyneux and Hill won the first race, and set the first ever 110mph lap. Afterwards one of the scrutineers came over and offered to tag the engine. This meant they would drill the cylinder head bolts, and then put a lockwire through it and a lead seal. They would then let the rider race in the second leg if that seal was intact, but if the seal was broken they would be excluded. Molyneux refused and insisted that the outfit went into the scrutineering bay there and then and that the officials took the cylinder head off as quickly as possible in order to inspect it. Rumours were still swirling about the paddock that the machine must be illegal in some way or form, even though it had already passed a fuel test. Not surprisingly, all was declared to be within the regulations. In truth the engine was not the greatest motor that had ever been used at the TT races, but it owed a lot to 'Slick' Bass, who had worked his magic on it. He had made it a good engine, but only through his ability as an engine tuner. It was not a good engine in itself, and Slick himself did not think that it would last the distance, which illustrates just how poor it was. This, as always, was down to finance, in that Molyneux did not have the money to put exotic parts into it. Instead, it was Bass's skill that got it home. Molyneux continues the story:

> Anyway that shut up all the backstabbers. It was legal and that was that. We went out for the second race and I was determined we were going to average over 110 miles an hour for the three laps on this one, never mind lap at it. And we did, we averaged over 110 miles an hour. We put the lap record up to over 111 miles an hour, and that was back in 1996. There are people today who struggle to do that speed, and I would say the track is three miles an hour faster today, easily. I sold the bike immediately. In fact a guy came to me wanting to buy that bike before the second race – after it had been declared all above board obviously! – but we agreed a price, he gave me a cheque, and I remember coming down towards the Creg on the last lap of the second race thinking, 'Keep going you bastard thing!!' It sounded like a bag of nuts and bolts! He bought that thing as seen, with no spares or anything, but I told him in no uncertain terms, 'You definitely need to get that engine rebuilt before you run it!' Well he couldn't resist it – he went out to Oulton Park the following week, for a short-circuit meeting and on his sixth lap the bloody conrod snapped and went out the front of the engine. A history-making engine destroyed, all because he couldn't be patient! Funnily enough though that bike is now out in New Zealand, a guy is running it out there, and it's still winning races after all these years.[37]

After the TT Molyneux sold the bike for what was probably a record amount. He named his price, and the buyer took it. Combined with his prize money, that meant he was sitting on about £20,000 altogether. This was enough to make a good impression in European racing, and so that was what Molyneux chose to do in 1997, thus missing the TT in that year. With the previous year's winner not attending, in 1997 Roy Hanks asked the organisers if he could use the vacant number 1 plate, to which they agreed. Race 1 saw Hanks take his first victory in three decades of racing at the TT, an emotional event for all concerned. He remembered afterwards:

> When you finish a race, you've normally got an idea where you've finished. Norman, my elder brother, knew it was so close that a win was possible. I got a sign at the Bungalow on the last lap with a two and question mark beside it. What they were trying to tell me was that I might be first, but of course I thought it meant I was second or third. I've always said that people can put what they like on the pit-boards, I'm already trying my best, so it doesn't make much difference. So I just relaxed and drove as normal and it paid off. I know from Vince (Biggs, 2nd placed man) that he made some mistakes on the last lap because he was being distracted over what was written on his pit-boards. As I drove up the return road at the Grandstand, I was put straight into the winner's enclosure and I was amazed that I was the only one in there, because Rob Fisher passed us early on in the race. We passed Rob after he'd broken down, but I was concentrating that hard

I didn't even see him. From there on in, everyone was congratulating us and it was amazing. Even Mick Boddice did, and we're not the best of mates, me and Mick. He came up and said 'About bloody time!' and walked off again: that's all he said![38]

For Race 2, Rob Fisher and Rick Long, whose engine had overheated in the previous outing, were the favourites to win. They had been quickest in practice, and had produced the fastest lap in the first race before dropping out. As before, Hanks with passenger Phillip Biggs was first off the line, but by Ballacraine Fisher had caught them on the road, and corrected time put him in the lead. By the last lap, Fisher had opened up a gap of over a minute between himself and the rest of the field. After cruising to a commanding victory he commented:

Winning a TT is a major achievement. We've finished and we've won, and we're delighted [even if] we didn't win the double.[39]

Molyneux was back at the TT, and scored another win in 1998. It was a big year for Honda, the fiftieth anniversary of the founding of the company. Honda UK general manager Bob McMillan was a big personality, and he was determined that Honda would win every major class at the TT that year, and turn the Isle of Man into 'Honda Island' in celebration. He sat down with Molyneux to discuss what he would need if he were to ride in the company colours, and it became the beginning of a partnership that would last nine years. Molyneux came away from the meeting with an agreement that Honda would supply him with race engines, spares and a budget to look after them. The only thing Molyneux was afraid to ask for was a cash retainer. This particular year Race Week was beset with bad weather, leading to the first sidecar race being cancelled. All of the prize money from the first race was added to that of the second, making it a handsome sum for the eventual winner. However, Molyneux had made himself unpopular by giving an interview about the situation to a journalist from *Motorcycle News*, who had misquoted him to the effect that he thought half the field were holiday racers who stood no chance of winning the money in the first place! After this debacle he had difficulty showing his face in the paddock without attracting abuse, but a more serious problem was with his passenger, Doug Jewell. The two had just not gelled as a team during practice, and Doug was certainly not at ease with Molyneux's driving style. Molyneux describes the race:

> [It] wasn't a great event, for a variety of reasons. I'd still got passenger issues (Dougie was really uncomfortable on the bike and had actually told me at one point during practice that he wanted off the thing). So I had to ride with this in mind. I had to ride with a guy that didn't really want to be there. As bad luck would have it, the weather was atrocious. At the beginning of the race it was damp in some places, properly wet in others; there were leaves everywhere. I went off the start line, and I wouldn't say that my heart wasn't totally in it, but I was just so apprehensive going out to ride, because of both the

weather conditions and Dougie's insecurities on the bike. So I set about the race as best I could – but you can get an idea of how uncharacteristic it was for me from the fact that at the Hawthorn, Rob Fisher who set off at number 2 passed me – not in the real world would that ever happen! I'd set the quickest lap of practice, only several seconds short of the lap record, and Rob just wasn't on that kind of pace that year. He was on a mission now though, but I just thought, 'I've got to ride this race using my bloody head.' I knew the bike would finish, that went without saying. Even so, I had to think carefully how I treated this race, because I could either get a fist in my back, saying, 'I don't want to go round anymore Dave,' or I could go sideways into a bloody hedge because of the conditions. So I had a lot going on in my head, and that's without half the paddock wanting to put me up on a shooting range into the bargain!

Off I went, taking it steady, and once Fisher had passed me I just sat on his tail; I sat on his back tyre, and just before Sulby Straight a plume of smoke came out from the underneath of his bike. I thought to myself, 'That's it boy, you've popped it.' I was third when Fisher went out, and that promoted me up to second, and it was then it was just a matter of time really, just a case of plugging away. Once I knew Dougie was comfortable with going round how I was riding – and I wasn't getting any indication that he wasn't – we went on and won the race. Yes we won it, and yes we scooped up all that prize money, and yes we won it under Honda colours.[40]

But the reality of the situation was that at the Honda presentation afterwards when they called all of the winning riders up on stage to thank them, the others, the solo victors, were all professional riders on a Honda wage, whereas Molyneux was basically a privateer with Honda backing. But the even greater difference perhaps was that that his outfit, unlike the solos, had been built from scratch. In the greatest tradition of sidecar racing, some talented engineers had pulled together to build that outfit, on and off the Isle of Man. Above all, it was built in the British Isles, and not in Japan!

The Molyneux and Fisher duel continued in 1999; however, this time they shared the honours with a win each, Molyneux remembering:

> I got Craig Hallam on the side, he was young and talented, and also a good sidecar driver as well so he understood what the bike was doing a lot of the time. Between us we could pretty much iron out any problem that was going on with it. It's quite unusual for a passenger to be a driver as well, but that guy was also equally talented on a solo machine. He was a winner at national level on several different makes of motorcycle, so he was an exceptional character and a brave lad. With him as a passenger I knew I could go as hard as I could, there were no worries there. 1999 was another celebration year for Honda, it was their fortieth year of competing at the TT. I built another new bike, with a newer-generation Honda engine in it, an FX model. We were quickest by something like four miles an hour in practice. We absolutely dominated it. In fact we

came to within one and a half seconds of setting the first ever sub-twenty minute lap.[41]

This was a considerable achievement at the time, and indeed the sub-twenty-minute lap remained an aspiration for many other sidecar drivers for at least a decade after this. Molyneux remembered also that the Honda engine he was now using was far from cutting edge:

> In 1999 that was on an old carburettored bike, with a CDI ignition unit. It was so basic, it had restricted carburettors, everything. My race craft, and my whole way of thinking about riding, had changed now. I didn't think so much about winning, I just wanted to set the track alight, and be faster than anything else by a long way. I lost races through trying to be fastest, and trying something different. Winning now held less of an appeal for me; it sounds strange, but that had dwindled, although the appeal of riding around the course was still there. I just wanted to push the speed barrier as far as I could, to take it to another level. That did cost me races, I know.
>
> I enjoyed the first leg of the TT that year, it was an excellent race; we won it by a very wide margin. We set a lap record of 112.76 in that first outing. It was about two seconds slower than we'd done in practice, so I was a bit disappointed with <u>that</u>, as I would have thought we would have gone quicker, but anyway that was the way it was. The second race came and the oil filter housing split on the last lap of the event going down towards Handley's Corner,

spraying oil up all over us. That was the end of that. I had thought that the engine had blown up; it wasn't until we got home that we discovered what the problem was. Anyway, it wouldn't have changed the result, we couldn't have fixed it at the side of the road. But we were in a two-minute lead at that time, on the last lap of a TT, cake walking it. So it was disappointing that we broke down when we really had that race in the bag. Also I was a bit aggrieved that as a result we didn't get to go under the twenty minute barrier as I had hoped, and that then became my new goal, because we had found in practice that, 'Jesus, it's achievable.' We nearly got it that night, and we were almost there. But we didn't get it then, and for various reasons it didn't happen for a number of years afterwards.[42]

With the Manxman away on World Championship duty in 2000, another double win fell easily to Fisher, who now also had Honda factory backing. The first race was held on the Saturday of Race Week and began in damp conditions, which got steadily worse over the three laps as rain began to fall. The conditions led to a high rate of attrition with Ian Bell, Allan Schofield and John Holden all going out on the first lap. Fisher said afterwards:

> We were ready for the weather. Even with so many going out I didn't slow down. If you slow down you lose your concentration.[43]

Reliability proved to be a factor in Race 2, because Ian Bell's Yamaha R6-powered outfit led for most of the way. Fisher had opted to fit a new exhaust in the second race that gave more bottom end power at the expense of outright top speed. The decision appeared to be a bad one until Bell's engine blew on the last lap. Fisher added:

> I am really happy to do the double. I have to admit that I think Ian Bell had that second race in the bag, so we were really lucky to get it. I had a big slide at Glen Tramman.[44]

In 2001, the TT was cancelled due to the outbreak of foot and mouth disease in the UK. The authorities in the Isle of Man were worried that people who had been in contact with the disease in England might well be going on to farmland as spectators at the races, and that was a risk they just didn't want to take. The whole event was scrapped, for the first time since the Second World War. Molyneux was planning to compete in the TT again, and had a good sponsor lined up in the form of a South African friend who lived on the Isle of Man. In some ways, however, the cancellation was good, for both him personally and for Honda. He remembered:

> I'd built a new bike, which used Honda's first ever 600cc injection engine, and it has to be said it was not good. In sidecar trim it was pretty poor. The electronics package which came with it was in its most primitive state. It would only allow you to increase the fuelling to the engine by 30%, so it didn't have anything like enough fuel going into the thing. As time went on, later that year, you could buy various smaller add-on aftermarket parts

which allowed you to get that up to 100%, and get the machine to run better. With a sidecar, you have to remove the standard equipment which comes with the engine, like the airbox, and you have to change the fuel map, in order to get more fuel through, and this engine basically wouldn't allow us to do that. It was so dog slow that it was embarrassing. If we had gone out to do the TT with that engine it would have been a disaster. During that year I only rode the bike two or three times. The first time convinced me that this injection system was never going to work. After that, we converted back to our system of carburettors and CDI ignition. It went well then, but if the TT had actually been on we would not have got into it anyway. We would have run out of time, as it was so late in the year that we finally got some sort of decent performance out of that engine. Looking at it that way, it was a good thing that the TT didn't go ahead in 2001.[45]

The TT was back in 2002, and the first race was won by Rob Fisher and Rick Long. Fisher made it into the record books by scoring his ninth TT win, joining three other drivers – Mick Boddice, Dave Saville and Siegfried Schauzu – as the joint most successful sidecar racers up to that time. Fisher and Long took victory by twenty-one seconds from second-placed crew Ian Bell and Neil Carpenter, with Bell slowing his pace after hitting the kerb at Laurel Bank in the opening lap. Molyneux, who had been favourite to win prior to the event, was hampered by an injury to passenger Colin Hardman, who had been knocked off his road bike in a collision with a car on the morning of the race, and finished fourth, which was really a credit to Hardman's determination in the face of his injuries. After that fourth place result he spent some time recuperating, and a few days later was in better shape when they went out for Race B in the 2002 TT. They finished second in that outing, after dicing with Rob Fisher for most of the distance, and it was a thrilling race according to onlookers and spectators. Molyneux went out first, Fisher was second behind him, and caught and passed him on the road, but the battle continued the whole way round until Fisher and Long made it a double victory, cementing them as the dominant crew at that time and crowning Fisher as the most successful sidecar driver ever up to that point, with ten wins and three second places from fourteen finishes. However, the reign of the Fisher king would not last long, and 2002 was to be his final TT appearance.

Underdog Dave Molyneux unsurprisingly was still as hungry as ever. For him the TT was much more his livelihood, for his business was building Formula 2 sidecar outfits for other riders. Riding at the TT – and being successful in it – was as much about advertising his products as anything else, but sometimes the two did come into conflict. He continues:

> I built a new bike in the early part of 2003, but I didn't manage to get it finished in time for the TT – I had quite a few to build for other people – so my own got shoved to the back of the queue and didn't get completed until just before Practice Week. It was a real contrast with the situation in 2001, in as much as we had really got the engine sorted out now. We really had got it to go. Honda supplied the gear –

good bits were coming through from them thick and fast now, like race parts that they were updating – and I got Slick Bass tuning the engines again, he really got them going. We set them up on the carburettors, and the older-type ignition that we had in '99. Together with the chassis I had built we had a really good package together at that stage.

We were quickest in practice again, in every session, but we went out in the first race and the rear wheel bearing collapsed. It went going into Parliament Square in Ramsey, but I had felt that there was something which wasn't quite right with it early on in the lap, at Kirk Michael. I was losing my brake pedal, and that was down to the movement in the wheel bearings, which moved the brake disc, and pushed the brake pads back, so when I came to brake I had to pump the pedal. That was in the first lap, and we were leading the race when we broke down. We had it sorted out for the second race, but there was a lot of bad weather that day. It started out damp, and there was a lot of tooing and froing on the start line. The ACU didn't know whether to hold it back any longer or postpone it or whatever, but anyway in the end we went out, on slick tyres. The weather gradually got worse during the race, there was low cloud on the mountain and puddles on the road, but we won by a considerable amount.[46]

Victory in Race 1 had gone to Ian Bell, his only TT win but something he admitted meant more to him than British Championship success. However, the era of dominance of the sidecar TT by Manx drivers and passengers was beginning.

Chapter 5

Manx Monopoly

By the mid-1990s, Dave Molyneux had begun to establish himself as a force to be reckoned with in the TT races. Yet this is not the whole of the story, for early on in his racing career Molyneux decided to combine his skills from his day job as a mechanic and metal fabricator, with his knowledge of what really worked for him in a sidecar outfit.

Initially he faced some suspicion from parts suppliers, but with his growing confidence gradually his reputation as a sidecar constructor grew, and by the early twenty-first century he was also the leading constructor on the sidecar grid. Dave Molyneux Racing (DMR) outfits became highly respected among the racing fraternity. Without recourse to blueprints or plans, and using a simple jig, he welded together tubular steel to create the frame to which the wheels, fuel tank, engine and eventually the bodywork of a racing sidecar outfit would be attached. Through many years of trial and error he came to work out the optimum positions for placing these components, in order to make the machine handle and corner in the most effective way.

As well as influencing a whole generation of sidecar drivers with his thinking on what made a good sidecar chassis, how it should be constructed and out of what, his innovative approach to design and construction would result in some massive TT landmarks being established in the coming years. In the winter of 2003–04 in his unassuming workshop at Regaby outside Ramsey, Molyneux began work on a new machine that would both shake the world of sidecar racing at the TT, and which would have dramatic personal consequences for Molyneux himself.

Since 1998, Molyneux had enjoyed factory support from Honda Britain, and in the spring of 2004 the firm supplied him with a new powerplant – a 600cc fuel-injected engine, of the type found on the firm's CBR600 series, and it was in order to accommodate this engine that the new machine was built. Sidecar races at the TT were now run under Formula 2 regulations, which allowed for four-cylinder, four-stroke engines. Previous fuel-injected engines from Honda had not worked well in a sidecar outfit, but now a lot of early difficulties had been resolved, and the new engine promised to have awesome amounts of power. With support from local sponsor Martin Bullock, and Sulby man Dan Sayle as passenger, the combination of men and machine proved its potential at the 2004 TT. They were fastest in every practice session and took victory in both sidecar races with ease.

In Race A the Manx duo took control from the start line, and remained so throughout the three-lap outing. On the second circuit they reached 112.61mph, to come within an ace of the lap record (set by Molyneux in 1999). Even a rattle that developed within the engine and which forced them to slow on the last lap did not prevent them from winning by fifty-nine seconds, a truly commanding margin. In the second sidecar race of the meeting, Molyneux made it his third TT double in eleven years. This time he and Sayle went even faster, breaking the 1999 lap record with a best speed of 113.17mph on lap two. Only a badly blistered rear tyre forced them to relax the pace a little on lap three, Molyneux later telling *Motor Cycle News*:

> We had a couple of major slides so I knew the back tyre was going off.[1]

The final 'touring' lap allowed second-placed driver Nick Crowe to take almost twenty seconds out of their lead, but it was still another resounding victory for Molyneux and Sayle. Having won in a race time of one hour, one minute and 4.2 seconds, the magical sub-20-minute lap, a personal target that he had set himself back in 1999, seemed now to be almost within Molyneux's reach. However, despite all this early success with the new machine, 2005 opened with some difficulties. Practice Week was beset with mechanical problems, particularly surrounding the engine management system on the outfit. By the end of the week Molyneux, again with Dan Sayle in the chair, had not even qualified. He had done two untimed laps only in the first Saturday practice session, with constant breakdowns meaning that by the Friday he had yet to complete a timed lap. Molyneux later remembered:

> By the Friday night the pressure was really on, but we went out and did two laps under twenty minutes, the first time that had ever been done. I'd had a lot of earache during the week, people saying the pressure was on, and if we didn't qualify then we wouldn't be able to race, blah

blah blah. I just thought, 'Oh, give us a break.' We'd been out on the Saturday night, and did two laps with the bike straight out of the crate. We knew what speed we had done that night and so did they, but we'd still been getting these jibes thrown at us all week that we wouldn't be on the grid if we didn't get a lap of practice in that Friday night. Well we got those laps in, and I think it was Chris Kinley, the radio commentator, who came up to us afterwards and said, 'Dave, you've made history, the first ever sub-twenty-minute laps.' I was pretty cool about it and just said, 'Oh well, at least we've qualified!'[2]

However, the first sidecar race of the 2005 TT was a less than auspicious occasion, with poor weather contributing to the difficulties experienced by the crews. The road was damp, indeed at times during the race it was actually raining. Nevertheless Molyneux set a blistering pace right from the flag, putting in a first lap at nearly 110mph, from a standing start in wet conditions. In the long run, however, the Regaby man was to fall victim to the same technical problems that had dogged him during practice. A plug cap coil had burned out, and the engine began to misfire on one cylinder. The Manx duo pulled in and retired, at a point in the race in which they held a forty-five-second lead, one of the biggest in Molyneux's career. It was a disappointing result to say the least, but again the sheer speed of the outfit was clear to see. The lead in the race was picked up by fellow Manx duo Nick Crowe and Darren Hope, who scored their first TT win. Crowe, who had started out as a sidecar passenger in the early 1990s but who switched to driving in

2001, would become the dark shadow behind Molyneux for the next four years, snapping at his heels and eager to exploit any chance of success.

Between races, Molyneux was able to identify and finally fix the technical gremlin that had caused so many problems, and in a final lap of practice before Sidecar Race B the potential of this machine showed itself quite clearly, with a time once again under twenty minutes. The 2005 Sidecar B race was an electrifying affair, with Molyneux and Sayle putting in three laps each under twenty minutes, with the first ever sidecar race average of under an hour and setting a 116mph lap record into the bargain. This amazing feat was achieved in spite of the fact that on the final lap (and almost within sight of the Grandstand) a wheel bearing had collapsed, meaning that the machine had to be coasted in and across the line to take its third TT win.

From its first arrival in 2004 the Honda fuel-injected 600cc unit had the potential to be explosive, but in combination with the chassis that Molyneux had built to house it, and with the refinements and developments he had made over the course of two years, everything had by now come together into an outstanding package. He had no reason to think that 2006 would not bring further refinements and even greater power and speed, and the early part of that year certainly gave every indication that this would be the case. Now with former passenger Craig Hallam back aboard, the pairing began the season by contesting short-circuit meetings in England. Molyneux recalls:

> We won the first two rounds of the British [Formula 2 Sidecar] Championship by a street mile, and when we went

into the TT that year we were leading the Championship. It's really not an exaggeration to say that at that particular point in time we were in a different league from everyone else. Wet or dry conditions, it made no difference; there were guys there who professed to be wet-weather specialists, but we just blasted past them, in fact Craig said to me at one point, 'This is ridiculous, it's too easy Dave.' So we went into the TT in a strong position … [3]

With engine refinements and tuning by Dave Hagen of Evomoto, the DMR 600cc outfit again promised fireworks. The two engines supplied by Honda used standard parts, but Hagen's modifications were designed to wring extra ounces of power from them. One such change involved modifying the crankcases, by making holes so that the bottom end breathed better as the pistons rose and fell. Baffles were also fitted in the sumps to reduce oil starvation. Unlike the engine of a solo outfit that leans into a bend, in a sidecar engine centrifugal force on a corner tends to drive the oil to one end of the sump and away from where it is needed. It is well known that fitting baffles in the sump can reduce this effect, and the consequent engine wear and tear. Other modifications, however, remain closely guarded secrets in the competitive world of the race engine tuner.

Sure enough, the Molyneux outfit continued to rip up the record book at the 2006 TT. On the Wednesday evening of Practice Week, it set a new lap record from a stationary position; the achievement was all the more incredible because a standing start would normally mean giving away anything between ten and fifteen seconds on a flying lap, but the machine completed

Right: Manx passenger Arthur Kinrade, seen in the mid-1920s. (Courtesy of Vanda Murray)

Below: Winners of the 1925 sidecar TT race: Len Parker of Oldfield Park, Bath and passenger K.J. Horstman of Newbridge Hill, with the Mercury trophy awarded by the ACU. (Author's Collection)

Above: Eric Bliss, Eric Oliver, Cyril Smith and Stan Dibben at the 1955 TT. (Courtesy of Manx National Heritage PG/12100/2)

Left: Walter Schneider, winner of the 1955 sidecar TT race, with the ACU trophy. (Courtesy of Lothar Mildebrath)

Above: Manfred Grunwald, who was passenger for Fritz Hillebrand between 1954 and 1957. (Author's Collection)

Below: Bill Beevers and passenger John Chisnall calmly awaiting the start of the 1960 sidecar TT. A lot of detail on Beevers' BMW outfit is visible, including the Rennsport frame, and the passenger handles on the Watsonian platform. (Courtesy of John Chisnall)

Above: It looks worse than it is – Heinz Luthringshauser's outfit overturning while on fire in a crash at Quarter Bridge in the 1963 TT. Both men escaped with minor injuries. (Courtesy of Ranscombe Brothers Photographic)

Below: Max Deubel and Emil Hoerner (first), Colin Seeley and Wally Rawlings (second), and Georg Auerbacher and Benedik Helm (third) on the podium in 1964. (Courtesy of Josef Ried)

Above: Derek Yorke and passenger John Chisnall, prior to the 1966 TT. The Triton outfit combined a superior Triumph engine with a Manx Norton frame. (Ray Horsnell, courtesy of John Chisnall)

Right: Passenger Dane Rowe, who appeared at the TT between 1968 and 1972. Several times she competed alongside her husband, Swiss engineer and driver Rudi Kurth. (Author's Collection)

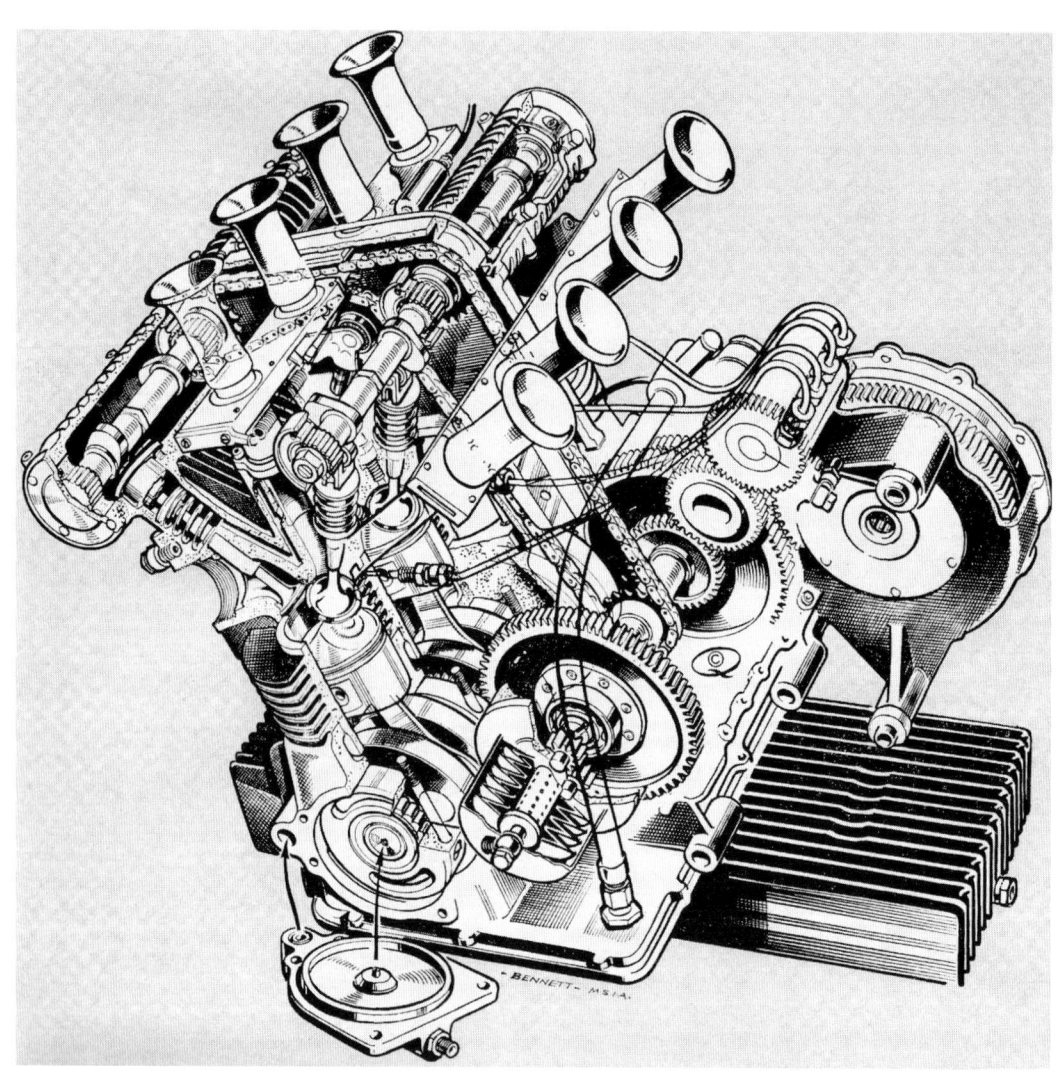

A diagram of Fath's URS engine. (Author's Collection)

Above: Australian sidecar champion Alex Campbell with his outfit at the Sea Terminal, Douglas, in 1975. (Courtesy of Manx National Heritage PG/13633/1/1975/445/1)

Below: Schauzu and Dieter Busch, early 1970s. (Courtesy of Josef Ried)

Left: Georg Auerbacher lifts the Fred Dixon Trophy at the Villa Marina, following victory in the 1971 750cc race. (Courtesy of Josef Ried)

Below: George O'Dell and Kenny Arthur after victory in the 1977 sidecar Race A. (Courtesy of Christine Arthur)

the circuit some two seconds under Molyneux's previous best time. The lap was timed officially at nineteen minutes twenty-eight seconds, amazingly fast. It seemed at that time that nothing could match this outfit, or indeed prevent it from easily claiming another two TT wins. The following evening the duo went out again, not with the intention of breaking any lap records, but merely to make sure they had given themselves the maximum possible amount of familiarisation time before Race Week. Molyneux recalls that night:

> So we set off with all new tyres and chain and brake pads, and by the time you get to Ballacraine all that stuff is bedded in, it's well and truly bedded in, and so you can light the thing up a bit, start to go a lot quicker if you feel comfortable, and I'd never felt more comfortable in twenty years of racing round the TT mountain circuit than I did that night. I don't have a great recollection of what happened next that evening, or an understanding of why it happened.[4]

As the machine approached Rhencullen, between the fifteenth and sixteenth milestones beyond Kirk Michael village, all seemed normal. Molyneux took a tight line on the right-hander at the top of the hill, which was extremely bumpy but which gave a good line going into the next bend, a left-hander. However, as the bike approached the jump it became unstable, running on the edge of the front tyre and making it hard to control. At 140mph, as it went over the jump, the outfit flipped. Trapped underneath, Molyneux skidded down the road, fighting with the machine to free himself as he did so. As it hit a stone wall, he parted company with it, and staggered to his feet. In the minutes that followed, he stared back up the hill in disbelief, unable to comprehend what had just happened. When the bike eventually stopped sliding and dug in, it went end over end, righted itself and came to rest back on its wheels. In the dramatic events beforehand, however, it had been doused in high-octane race fuel; as it had travelled down the road, the top of the airbox had worn away, exposing the fuel rail, which had also come into contact with the road. The friction caused sparks that set the outfit instantly alight. With two laps' worth of race fuel still on board and highly flammable carbon fibre bodywork, it went up like a Roman candle. Passenger Craig Hallam was able to walk away with minor cuts and bruises, but after getting quickly out of the road for fear of being hit by the following outfit, Molyneux took stock of his own injuries, which were severe:

> I walked into a nearby garden, and a kind gentleman from the house came out to see if I was OK. I was holding my right arm [which] was four inches longer than it should have been, and it didn't feel as if it was connected somehow. I knew as well that I'd taken a heavy smash in the right shoulder, because it wasn't there, it was now inside my ribcage. The guy from the house looked as scared as anyone I've ever seen, poor guy, he'd seen the whole thing happen. The marshals must have been shocked at the incident as well, but they reacted amazingly. I take my hat off to the marshals because it's a hell of a job they've got

to do, and the concern on their faces after just witnessing a 140 mile an hour crash, and then the machine going on fire, was obvious. I heard one guy shouting, 'Where is he?' They must have thought I'd been fired over a hedge or something, but then they saw me in the garden. I could see the bike was burning fiercely now but I was resigned to the fact that there was nothing I could do about it.[5]

This incredible machine, which had achieved so much in such a short space of time, went on to become part of the collections of Manx National Heritage. Carefully preserved in the state it was left in on the day of the crash, it is a unique item unparalleled by any comparable object in a British motorsport museum. Looking beyond the obviously charred and blackened metalwork and fabric, evidence of the severity of the impact at Rhencullen that night is clearly apparent. The front brake disc is bent, and the fuel rail shows unmistakable scuff marks from contact with the road. It is, however, a testament to its builder's skill that the machine survived the impact largely intact, without breaking up. Molyneux for his part, sadly announced his retirement from racing. The decision was largely a financial one, with every penny more or less of his racing budget tied up in a machine that had just gone up in smoke. Yet within a few weeks things had taken on a different complexion, because two of his first visitors into hospital after the crash were Dave Hancock and Mark Davies. Davies had recently taken over from the legendary Bob McMillan as general manager of Honda UK, and Hancock was the firm's head of Research and Development; more than just sponsors, the two were his personal friends. When Molyneux told them that he thought that he was not going to be able to get back into racing because of the cost of getting things back on track, it was these two who pulled a deal together. It was their support that got his career going again.

With the red hot favourites now out of contention, the two sidecar races in the 2006 TT were taken by Manxmen Nick Crowe and Darren Hope. After a difficult Practice Week, Crowe's DMR Honda outfit was running smoothly by the time Race A came around, and in good conditions Crowe and Hope began to turn up the wick. On the first lap they quickly took the lead from main rivals Steve Norbury and Scott Parnell. As the race reached its halfway point, Crowe/Hope led Norbury/Parnell by seven seconds. Further back interest focussed on a battle between Roy Hanks/Dave Wells (with Roy at his fortieth TT), and John Holden/Andy Winkle. On their second lap Crowe and Hope became only the second crew ever to lap under twenty minutes, and were stretching their lead despite Crowe being in pain from a hand injury sustained in a crash at Scarborough a month earlier. By the end of the third lap they were twenty seconds ahead of the second-placed men and crossed the line with a forty-seven-second advantage. After minor incidents put out some of the front runners, Holden/Winkle managed third, and Hanks/Wells were well pleased with fourth place. Later, Crowe paid tribute to the help that he had received from the injured Dave Molyneux. He was delighted with the result, adding:

> We would have been quicker on the last lap except for catching high number outfits. It was great and I'd like to

thank our sponsor Andy Faragher who has been absolutely marvellous. We started steadily as we weren't sure whether it would even go off the line after all the adjustments we had had to make. If Dave [Molyneux] had been in it we'd have been playing for second best. Let's hope we can change his mind about not doing the TT any more.[6]

Third-placed man Holden commented:

Our first board showed seventh, so I had to sort myself out a bit. Then we were fourth and took third when Simon [Neary] spilled. I'd rather have been third in my own right. It was really hot out there and I was worried about the temperature of the radiator. It was our first year with the Honda RR and I'll have to ask Nick for some advice.[7]

Race B presented a much greater challenge, however, for the Manx pairing. Difficulties with the DMR Honda's fickle engine management system meant that Crowe had to reset it virtually every mile during the race. In spite of the difficulties they were still leading Norbury/Parnell by over sixteen seconds at the end of the first lap. At Ramsey on the second lap, passenger Hope shook his head at radio commentator Roy Moore to indicate that all was not well with the engine, but even so by the Grandstand they had extended the lead to over twenty seconds! A suspected puncture caused Holden and Winkle to stop, thus promoting Hanks and Wells to third place, which they were able to hold, giving them a podium position. After crossing the line to take victory, Crowe told reporters:

> It was certainly annoying and quite hairy having to cope with the ECU fault. The on-board computer shuts the engine down completely but when it's reset the engine chimes in with a big bang. I must have had to do it 30 or 40 times a lap, and at Sulby second time I felt like pulling in and going home. When it did it at the bottom of Barregarrow on the last lap I thought we'd lost it completely but somehow we stayed aboard. If anyone had told me before the TT that I was going to do the double, I'd have said they were dreaming.[8]

His elation was almost as great as that of Roy Hanks, who joked that the stress and excitement of the race had caused his pacemaker to kick in. Hanks had been partnered with Dave Wells since 2000, but it was not an audacious start, Hanks recalling:

> Passenger-wise I ended up with Dave Wells, bless him. I never wanted him, as he was a Boddice-boy as far as I was concerned, and all of my passengers previously had been young. So they did what I wanted. I told Dave what I wanted and we had a nose-to-nose 'discussion'. He said: 'You drive it. I'll passenger it.' And we ended up getting on like a house on fire after that. We had 10 years together. Brilliant. We always had a lot of fun.[9]

Sadly the fun ended for Hanks when Dave Wells was later killed in an accident at Mallory Park, though he would race on at the TT for a few more years with Kevin Perry in the chair.

Meanwhile, staff at Nobles Hospital had told Molyneux that he would definitely need surgery, but they said that it could be up to nine months before they could do anything with the shoulder. They added that there would be a good three-month recovery period after that, but that would be recovery up to the point where he could then start to train and get fit. This in turn meant that at that point in time, racing in the TT centenary in 2007 would definitely be out of the question. Nobles had done a great job of putting the injured shoulder back together in the first place, but now the urgency that was driving Molyneux along was the need to get back into racing as quickly as possible. As well as having the dressings changed regularly at Ramsey Cottage Hospital, he was going to the hyperbaric chamber in Douglas every day to help heal the flesh wounds sustained in the crash – the hyperbaric chamber encourages the healing process by compressing the oxygen in the air, so that more is breathed in and absorbed by the body. While at the chamber one day someone suggested physiotherapy for the injuries, which led to an appointment with well-known physiotherapist Isla Scott, who specialised in sports injuries. This in turn led to a meeting with Dr Lennard Funk, a South African surgeon based in Manchester. He was initially worried that the injury was too complex, and that there was too much nerve damage, but agreed to go ahead with the operation. It was costly, but it was successful. If it had not been for Funk and Isla Scott then Molyneux would never have made it to the 2007 TT, it simply would not have been possible.

He started working again in January 2007. He managed at first about half a day at a time, and some days had to leave it and come back to it later in the day. A shoulder injury can prove one of the hardest to get over, because rather than being the socket that holds it together, the shoulder is connected by tendons and muscle and if they have been damaged, the arm is going to shake. In particular he found welding a struggle. Dr Funk had predicted that the effects of the injury would still be evident two years down the line, but Molyneux had to get on and build himself a new bike ready for that year's TT. The bike he had in 2006 was probably the best he had ever built. But with the new outfit that he had constructed early in 2007 things were different; the chassis was great, it would go around corners just like the old bike, but it simply wasn't as quick. It didn't accelerate as dramatically, it didn't get from A to B anything like as fast, and it was down on top speed considerably as well, which was purely down to lack of time with the new type of Honda engine. The Molyneux team did not get those new Honda engines until March of that year, so it left too small a gap to get things built while he was still struggling physically.

Passenger Rick Long was living in England at the time, so the technical side of things was falling heavily on Molyneux. Without the bike being ready, it could not be track tested, therefore they could not move on with the engine development, and as a result it was not a particularly good package if the truth is known. In fact, Molyneux candidly admitted later that it was one of the worst packages he had ever put together. No one was at fault, the only fault was that he had injured myself. Maybe if he had not, and they had just moved on to that newer-generation engine, then they would have had more time to work on that new power plant, and the machine might have been a lot better. He would certainly have been fitter, and would also have had more confidence, because that had also taken a knock as a result of the crash. The upshot of all this was that Molyneux and Long missed the first practice of the TT that year, simply because the bike wasn't ready. Molyneux remembers:

It's fair to say though we had a disastrous practice week in 2007, one of the worst. We missed the first practice session on the Saturday because we were still getting the bike ready. We went up to Jurby airfield on the Sunday to test it; we had a brand new race engine in, and when we ran it one of the conrod bolts broke. The conrod went out of the front of the engine, and this brand new engine was instantly destroyed. We only had two tuned engines and now one of them was wrecked. We wanted to have the other tuned engine which we had sat there checked over, to make sure that there was nothing loose or wrong there as well, so we had that one stripped down. Meanwhile, one of our sponsors paid for a brand new CBR600 road bike from Tommy Leonard's dealership, and we pulled the engine straight out of that and put it in the outfit, just so that we could go out on the Monday night for practice. We just did a slow lap of practice, we just toured round that night but the suspension was all wrong so that needed some more work. It turned out that our other tuned engine was fine so we put that back in, went out on the Tuesday night with it, and an ignition sensor broke on it. I think it was Wednesday night before we really seriously got going. On Thursday we put a quick lap in, but we'd had a dreadful week and were something like ten horsepower down on our 2006 bike, which is massive, a huge amount.[10]

Clive Padgett, the motorcycle dealer and sponsor from Batley, was well known for helping sidecar teams as well as running his own solo operation. He lent Molyneux and his crew a Motec engine management system, and a wiring loom. However, the wiring loom is made to go on a solo, not a sidecar, so it was not going to be a case of simply slotting it in. Clive said that they could borrow this item of kit, but only after practice week. Fortunately, the organisers postponed the first sidecar race on the Saturday, and that gave them time. Molyneux went straight round to Clive, got the item and then spent all night on it. Instead of going to bed on Saturday evening, he spent all night fitting the management system and altering the wiring loom and the clock set to go on it. The following morning they went out at Jurby airfield to set it up, and eventually got it going, but the outfit was still way off the pace. Molyneux describes his first outing in anger aboard the machine:

> We went off in the first race, and with our lack of power I knew that it was just a matter of time before Nick Crowe came past us, which he did. But then he had an engine problem of some description, and went out, and at that point I thought 'Right, get your head down.' With all that had gone on I was bit deflated though, I wasn't myself at all. That crash the previous year definitely had an effect on how I was thinking and feeling, but so did the practice

week. It was far from being a good team effort. Anyhow at that point in the race I saw we had a board saying we were third, and then I got another board saying we were second and that was at half distance. It was halfway round the second lap, and I thought, 'F***king come on,' I remember properly shouting at myself inside my helmet, shouting, 'Pull your f***king finger out!' and off we went whoosh, and we won it from John Holden by something like five seconds.[11]

The two HM Plant Honda solo riders that year, John McGuinness and Ian Hutchinson, had one spare CBR 600cc engine to share between them. In the intervening spell between that first sidecar race and Race B it came to a point where they knew they would not need it, so Neil Tuxworth the Honda team manager offered it to Molyneux, as the engine was just sitting in a corner. He accepted Tuxworth's offer and fitted it to the outfit, but it was hard to say if it went any better than what they already had in place.

Race B came around and with it came another incident blown up by the press. Molyneux and Long got into the warming up area, and the rev counter – the clock set – started jumping around with the gauge going up and down. Nick Oldfield, who assisted the team with wiring, was there and identified it as a loose connection. He ran off, got a soldering iron, stuck it in, and it was sorted, or so it seemed. They got out onto the grid, the three-minute board went up, and the clock started going haywire again. Molyneux asked his brother Graham to run down and get another clock, so he hot-footed it down to the paddock, came back with the spare, by that time the first one was off and they put the other one on. In the meantime, however, the organisers had announced a five-minute delay in starting the race because marshals were trying to catch a dog that was running loose on the track! With typical press exaggeration journalists wrote afterwards that this dog had saved Molyneux's race, and that if he was an animal lover he would have adopted it, along with other largely speculative comments. The bike would have operated 100 per cent efficiently with the first clock in place, and the only thing the driver would not have been able to see was how many revs the engine was producing and what temperature it was running at. It was not an essential part, and the driver would not look at it half of the time in any case. There was probably not a single rider there on the grid who would not have gone out just because that component was not working properly; furthermore Molyneux had already started unscrewing it when the five-minute delay was shouted out. Yet some people asserted that the delay was actually arranged deliberately to help him out of a fix. The strangest aspect of this story was one that was never reported at the time – that the outfit was actually technically illegal because it had within the background field of the race number a small sticker, a gift from a friend. This contravened the regulations, but no one seemed to have noticed. The subject of the sticker? A small cartoon dog. Molyneux takes up the story again:

> Anyway, we got away at the start of the race and it was a similar story to the first outing of that TT. Nick Crowe was streaking away with it for the first two laps, but

sidecar racing is as much about tactics as anything else, and sometimes when you go for speed you sacrifice reliability, that's the trade-off. I just thought, 'I'll keep my head down and ride my race, and see what happens.' Back in early 2006 we had been leading the British Championships. Wet or dry track, we were miles ahead. We were more than just dominant then, we were streets ahead of the rest of the pack. Maybe as a result of that we were over-confident at that point, I don't know. I do know that we went into that 2006 TT full of confidence, we ended up having an accident, the outcome was carnage, and I don't think I've been the same kind of rider since then … I just kept the pressure on Crowe, he knew I was behind him pushing him, and sure enough on the last lap at Ballahutchin he blew his engine. I came in to take my thirteenth win at the TT, and it was a historic moment, taking a double victory in the 100th anniversary of the event.

So having overcome all of that I feel quite proud of the fact that we won those two races at the 2007 TT. We won those races purely because we finished them. I suppose that year changed my outlook a little bit on how you win a race. In the past I was always hell bent on wanting to set the track alight, to be the fastest, but sometimes things have to be dealt with in a different way. If the bike ain't good enough then you're not going to be the quickest thing out there, but in spite of that we still achieved two wins at the Centenary of the TT. It will always be there in history, set in stone.[12]

The 2007 TT, however, was the high watermark of Molyneux's relationship with Honda. Shortly afterwards he parted ways with the Japanese manufacturer. In part it was the fact that it was getting harder for him to get the level of support that he needed as personnel changed within the company, and in part he did not feel that the newer generation of Honda engine was the right thing for a sidecar. It was true that others continued to use them successfully, and in fairness they were very fast, but it took a lot more work to make them that fast. For the 2008 season Molyneux had taken the unusual step of choosing to ride a Suzuki rather than a Honda-powered outfit. With the ups and downs of his life both on the track and away from it in the preceding few years, he felt that he needed a completely fresh start and a new focus. In fact, in racing terms it was a radical change. He commented:

> I decided to drop the Honda thing and go with something that I knew would be bloody hard work but which would give me a new challenge, and that was to go with Suzuki. I thought, 'Move on, and get the Suzuki engine.' No one had ever won a sidecar TT on one, and I wanted to try and do it. The Suzuki powerplant wasn't exactly an unknown quantity, however, there were numbers of other competitors using that engine at the TT and doing pretty well with it. But I don't tend to look at my nearest rivals, and wonder what they are doing, because they are the people I want to beat! I tend to look a lot further afield to see what the trends are. I look at the World Championship series, and the World Supersport Championships, and the

most powerful bikes are the ones at the front! Back at the TT, the TAS Suzuki team were winning races using the Suzuki 600cc engine, which was the one I was thinking about using.

I got in touch with Suzuki GB, and told them I was planning to run the Suzuki engine in my TT outfit. I told them it was something I fancied doing and I wondered if they were interested in joining up with me and giving me a bit of support, which they did. They were interested straight away. I had a meeting with some of the top people there, and they supplied me with race kit parts, things like that to put together this new bike. I think that Suzuki GB backed me, and gave me the gear, because they were desperate for some wins. They'd had a dry period, and apart from perhaps Bruce Anstey in the Superstock they hadn't got their name on the trophies much in the previous few years.[13]

However, the story of the sidecar TT races in the early 2000s was in two parts, both interconnected – that of the almost total dominance of the TT by Manx drivers Molyneux and Nick Crowe, and also of the rivalry between them, which was growing in intensity. No one, however, could have predicted how that would eventually end. Crowe reflected in 2008:

I was very determined to win last year especially with it being the 100th year. It was very disappointing to walk away with nothing. Not a cup or a memento. To get the lap record was a bit of a boost though. To lap as fast as we did in Centenary year was pretty satisfying when I think about it now. This year I definitely want to turn it around and win. Dave Molyneux knows he hasn't got it all his own way here now.[14]

That year Crowe had support from businessman Andy Faragher, owner of A. & J. Groundworks, as well as a major headline sponsor – having picked up the Honda package following the departure of Molyneux – and a new passenger in the person of Kent's Mark Cox, who had started his racing career as a solo rider before converting to the chair position. Crowe continued:

You know I could count on the fingers of one hand the passengers in world sidecar racing who I would be comfortable with, and confident in going at the pace I want to race at and Mark is one of those. When I heard he might be free for this season I gave him a call and jumped on the bandwagon before everyone else did … The Honda backing this year will be a real bonus and has put a whole new buzz around the team.[15]

Crowe was running the same LCR chassis as the previous year but with a new engine configuration and gearbox, the engine being set up for road racing in that it produced a lot of power in a straight line. Once again the TT promised to be a true battle of the giants, though Molyneux (back with Dan Sayle on the side) was having teething troubles as might be expected with new machinery. He only got to race once before the 2008 TT, at Jurby road circuit, and the bike handled very differently from what he was used to because of the way the engine was situated in the chassis. He then went into the TT with the new Suzuki outfit, but it was a difficult scenario because it was a totally new thing to him, and completely out of his comfort zone. Realistically, he had put too much onto his plate in expecting to win when the reality was that he never ridden with that engine before, and the chassis was also radically different in order to accommodate that new motor. He continues:

> We had a tough practice week in 2008, with constant electrical faults. It turned out that the Motec engine management system we used wasn't compatible with a lot of Suzuki's own electrical sensors. It was something we only found out during practice week, that over a long distance like the TT course these components got hot and started to break down. If you could pit stop for a new sensor every lap it would have been fine but we couldn't! It took us all week to try to sort these problems out and even by race week we still hadn't fully got to grips with them. We broke down in the first race because we'd had an engine fault right in the last practice session, on the night before the first race, and we'd been up till three in the morning trying to sort this fault out. The engine was then put back together out of two other engines to try and get around this fault, and in the process of reassembling it the clutch didn't go back together correctly. We had no time to test it, we had to go straight out onto the grid on the following morning, and the clutch slipped as soon as we set off from the line.[16]

Crowe for his part stormed ahead to take his fourth TT victory. He chased early leaders John Holden and Andy Winkle for most of the first lap and only at the halfway stage, approaching Ballaugh Bridge, did he manage to pass them on the road, before extending his lead to win by nineteen seconds. Afterwards he told reporters that he had struggled somewhat, as the engine was not as fast as he expected it to be. He repeated the feat in Race B, in a battle that was as much against the conditions, in particular the prevailing high winds, as against other riders. Crowe led from the start but Molyneux battled his way up from third to second. The two were then neck and neck for the rest of the race, but Crowe managed to hold on to his ten-second advantage. Crowe commented afterwards:

> We had a good time up there, me and Dave [Molyneux] rode our arses off. I think we were even touching at times, I'm made up. I got a good run, it wasn't handling the best, I think we made the wrong tyre choice.[17]

Passenger Cox added:

> It was awesome, better than the first. Dave pushed us all the way. Water started pouring out on the second lap and I was just praying that it would hold out. I was expecting Moly to come past but all credit to Nick.[18]

That year also saw the debut at the TT of Sidecar World Champion Tim Reeves, who continued a trend that had started back in 2004, when another World Champion, Austrian Klaus

Klaffenböck, had fulfilled his dream of finally racing on the Mountain circuit. Reeves had his first taste of the TT as a spectator in 2006, when he also helped out with pit boards for Steve Norbury. Initially, racing the TT was not on Reeves' agenda as while competing in the World Championships it would have required a different type of machine and a second additional budget to run it. While his backers were generous, a proposition like this would have been stretching things too far!

However, having won three consecutive world titles between 2005 and 2007, Reeves was ready for a new challenge and with support and encouragement from Paul Phillips at the Isle of Man Government Motorsport Office, was able to put a package together for the 2008 TT. Steve Webster, who marketed LCR components in the UK, was keen for him to participate, and supplied a free LCR chassis to kick-start Reeves' campaign. He was meticulous in his preparation, remembering:

> I just focussed on doing everything very professionally. If you really want to do something, and do it well, you have to put the right amount of effort in. I think anything is achievable if you prepare right so that's what I tried to do. I did about 35 laps in a car just to learn where the road goes, but it doesn't become real until you go out there on the bike. Once I was comfortable where the road went left and went right I started thinking about racing lines and so on.[19]

The Crowe-Molyneux rivalry continued into 2009, with the former continuing to have official Honda support. During

Practice Week Crowe and passenger Cox experienced mechanical issues on both the Monday and Tuesday night sessions, causing them to pull up on both occasions, although they managed to post the fastest lap of practice. Molyneux was also having problems as he continued to iron out the gremlins in the Suzuki outfit, remembering:

> That bike [in 2008] was as good as it was going to be at that time, but it was still far short of its real capability, and I knew that potentially it was capable of a lot more. I then did several short-circuit meetings, but in the twelve months which followed I think I only did eleven races. Nevertheless, we developed the bike over that time, got rid of the Motec engine management system and went for one of Suzuki's own engine management systems. That worked a hell of a lot better … we went back to the TT in 2009 … on the run-up to the event a local businessman, Andy Faragher, had stepped in to support us with some finance, to help us get a more competitive package together. We got two new engines together, and had them race tuned, but the advice that the tuner took from what was considered to be a reliable source turned out to be wrong. Really through no fault of his own the tuner had been given wrong information, and as a result these two engines which had been paid for by Andy Faragher turned out not to be up to much. In preparation for the event we'd also had some other engines that had failed. They were fast, but they'd failed. So in the weeks prior to the TT we'd had fast engines that had failed, and slow engines which

had also failed. We thought, 'What the hell do we do?' Well it was a joint decision by myself, Dan Sayle and my brother Graham to just do something between us, so we took these engines, stripped them down, and took what we thought were the best parts of each, put them all together and created this one engine which turned out to be not only reliable but fast as well. We went on to win Race A in the 2009 TT and to set the existing race record, over 115 miles an hour over three laps. None of us are engine builders or tuners, but there was a lot of common sense going on there. It made sense to us the way we put that engine together, and the guy I sold the bike to is still using that engine, it's still going strong, so something was very right there, it was a beautiful bike to ride ... [we] won it on that bike with a Suzuki engine and set a new race record. That was a great experience, because starting out with a brand new venture and producing a bike which could win the TT after only eleven outings was a pretty good achievement. Being realistic, that's an incredibly short space of time to get a new package up to that standard, but there are no shortcuts.[20]

The reliability problems that had dogged Cox and Crowe throughout Practice Week had continued into the first race, and they had broken down on the second lap at Greeba Bridge. After that, the scene was set for Race B to be an absolute show-stopper, and it had the makings of a classic head-to-head battle on the roads. It certainly set out that way, but unfortunately never reached a conclusion. In the second outing, Molyneux and Sayle started at number 2 and Crowe/Cox started as number 1. The race was flagged away at 6.15 pm and the two crews were almost equal in terms of speed, jousting on the road. The first indications of a problem, however, occurred at 6.28 pm when Molyneux and Sayle passed the transponder point at Ballaugh Bridge, but Crowe and Cox had disappeared from the live timings. Initial suspicions among fans fell upon the reliability issues that the duo had faced all week, but at 6.30 pm the race was red flagged, indicating a serious incident. Molyneux describes the scene as he encountered it:

> I remember coming around Alpine Corner, and just getting myself back to the centre of the road going past Ballakern Farm, when I saw a blanket of white smoke going down towards Ballacob. My first thought was, 'Nick's engine has blown up again.' So I dabbed the brake and rolled the throttle just to ease off, and the next thing I saw was a piece of his fairing floating down out of a tree; I knew that it was bodywork, and that was the first indication I had that something was seriously wrong here. Now I stood on the brakes, went through the gears and brought the machine down. There was less than ten seconds between us and Crowe on the road, so there was barely any reaction time. There would certainly have been no time for any of the marshals to react, because it was all just too quick. So there were no flags out, and we were literally on top of the scene of this accident within seconds of it happening. On entering into the smokescreen we saw that there were pieces of burning bike all over the road. Nick was laying in

the middle of the road, and I passed within a couple of feet of him. I couldn't see his passenger Mark Cox anywhere, but the bike was scattered all over the road. It really did resemble what I imagine an aircraft crash to look like. There wasn't a clear path through the debris at all, and the bike was thump-thumping over pieces of wreckage as we went on. I toured through the scene of the accident but as I did so Dan Sayle gave me a slap on the back, and gestured at me to crack on. It came into Dan's mind before it came into mine that there were bikes following us, and the smokescreen might well have cleared by the time they arrived on the scene; oblivious to what had happened they could easily race on through, and plough into the wreckage and into us if we were only touring.

I think I'd got to Ballaugh Bridge before I picked up the pace again. I suppose with hindsight I should have stopped there to inspect my own bike for any damage which it might have sustained from the debris in the road, but I had a lot going on in my head at that point. As you can imagine, when you've just seen something like that it takes a while to sink in. One thing I did have fixed in my mind though was there was no way that in the next twenty minutes that amount of carnage could be cleared up, not by any number of marshals, so I had a strong feeling that the race was going to be stopped; I didn't particularly feel like racing on anyway at that point. I picked up the pace a little bit and got into Ramsey, and it was at that point coming up out of Ramsey Hairpin that we saw the first yellow flag. As we were first on the roads I couldn't imagine that there was anything in front of us to slow us down, so I could only connect this to the crash. I suspected we were going to be pulled in. As we got up on to the mountain every single marshalling point had yellow flags out, so there was no doubt by now that the race was going to be stopped, and I knew that the Bungalow was the only place at which they could pull in a lot of bikes at once. We got up to the Veranda, and as I approached I could see a red flag being held out ahead of us, but at that point John Holden and Tim Reeves – who were in a personal battle – came racing past me, only to see the red flag ahead of them. They had quite a tussle going on, and they must have thought that the yellow flags were to indicate that I was having problems, and that was why I was touring. So we were all pulled over at the Bungalow, and when all the bikes were gathered up there we were allowed to proceed at a touring pace back to the Grandstand. There wasn't much else for it but to hope that the accident wasn't as serious as it looked, but it turned out that it bloody was. Those guys were lucky not to have been killed.[21]

The families later released a statement revealing that the accident was believed to have been caused by a collision with a hare. After nearly an hour of treatment at the roadside, the injured riders were airlifted to Noble's Hospital, where they remained for several days, before transfer to Liverpool for further medical attention. A later statement confirmed that doctors had been forced to remove the lower part of sidecar star Nick Crowe's right arm and insert donor bones in his right leg, and Cox also had to undergo bone insertion surgery. Later, in August, it was confirmed that Crowe had undergone four operations and was now mobile, albeit using a wheelchair. Cox had his pelvis, right hip and right arm repositioned, plated and pinned. He was not yet mobile, but later that month the pair were well enough to visit the Manx Grand Prix before returning to Liverpool for further treatment. A fundraising campaign was also organised by the families and this generated some money to help them re-adjust to life. Crowe in particular was determined to remain involved with sidecar competition and just a few years later would establish his own team, with Simon Neary and later Tim Reeves racing under his banner.

Molyneux was back at the TT in 2010, but this time the machine he had chosen to ride was Kawasaki-powered. The move came through personal interest rather than ambition, or through following the lead of others. He had decided that he was going to use the Kawasaki engine anyway, regardless of whether or not he could obtain any sort of factory backing, and it was for three main reasons: one, he had never won on this make before; two, his father and George Oates had raced on Kawasakis in the 1970s, and three, Kawasaki had never won in the sidecar class at the TT up to that point. So his aim was purely to win on that particular brand and make it successful. As it happened, Kawasaki were interested enough to provide him with an engine free of charge, which was a bonus, but they did not have a racing budget with which to put finance into it. After the TT that year he reflected:

I got in touch with Kawasaki UK, and told them, 'Look I've bought myself this engine, I'm building this new bike around it, I felt like I'd not nothing to lose by giving you a call to see if you wanted to help, and to be involved in this thing,' and they were dead keen straight away. Their presence at the TT has fluctuated over the years, but then they are the smallest of all the Japanese manufacturers ... I think, luckily for me, they are coming into a period where their product is doing very well. And it is luck because they did have lean years in the recent past, because their product hasn't maybe been quite as good as some of their competitors. But right now in Supersport 600 and in Superbike they've got some seriously good equipment, and riders want to ride that bike. So I think they are in a great position at the moment to do very well in the domestic scene, in the world scene and at the TT. I think that it's obvious when you see Ryan Farquhar and Conor Cummins going as well as they do in the solo classes at the TT. We proved a point as well with this Kawasaki engine at the 2010 TT, we got the fastest lap of practice, fastest lap of the event, and barring my own mistakes we really could have won that TT. That's why I would like if I could to go back and put that right, because we can do it ... Already, after the one TT that I've done on it, a couple of top teams have all of a sudden started using Kawasakis, just because of what we did in this TT.

... My current bike, the Kawasaki is fantastic. I'd say it handles equally as well as my old bike. On paper, I'd say it's got more power, but there are still things about it that I need to gel together. In 2010 I think I would rather have not done the TT at all than to have done it without trying new that Kawasaki engine. All of a sudden I've got a new ambition. No one ever in the history of the TT has won the sidecar event on all four Japanese makes of motorcycle. We've won on Yamaha, Honda and Suzuki, and now I want to add Kawasaki to that list. Added to that, no one has ever won a sidecar TT on a Kawasaki, just as no one had won on a Suzuki before last year. We were the first ones to do that. Now I feel that Patrick Farrance, who's an ex-World Champion passenger, is probably better in his application than I am in mine. I had somebody there riding next to me who is excellent, one of the best in the world, and we've both got the same ambition. He's never won a TT, and I've never won one on a Kawasaki, and I want to. We went into it having done only three short-circuit meetings in 2010, and we set the quickest lap of practice. All but for a bad choice of tuning on the engine, which was my choice, I feel that we really should have won that first race. But it was my decision to do what we did to the engine, and it was wrong, it was very wrong! It was wrong to the point where I actually wondered what the hell I'd done. But you can't just stop and put it right, you've got to ride through it.[22]

As it was, Race 1 in 2010 went to Honda-powered Klaus Klaffenböck, aboard an LCR framed outfit. Nicknamed 'Klaffi', the Austrian rider told the press after his win:

This means everything to me ... When I finished competing in the world championships in 2003 and came to the TT my target was to win this race. I immediately realised that would not be easy. Now I have done it, it feels mega.[23]

His passenger, Manxman Dan Sayle added:

I've been teaching him all week and we've even been going out for extra laps in the van after practice talking our way through various parts of the course. Klaus took it all in, he was spot on today.[24]

In Race 2 that year the leaders for much of the distance, John Holden and Andy Winkle, had to settle for second place. At the foot of the descent from the Mountain on the last circuit Klaffi snatched the lead from the Lancashire–Staffordshire duo, and managed to hang on to it for the remainder of the lap to take the chequered flag. The Austrian driver was elated afterwards, telling journalists:

That win means more to me than the first one. My boards kept reading -10, -10, -10, so I thought maybe I was sleeping for the first two laps. I didn't believe we could catch that gap up so when I finished I did not know if I was first, second or third. I tried all I knew and it worked. It won't really sink in until I get home to my wife and twin girls. It will make me very proud.[25]

For Sayle it was his sixth win in as many years and confirmed him as the best passenger of his generation. He too was elated with the result, announcing:

> I didn't really think we would get higher than third after a steady start. Klaus went a bit wild on the second lap and made a lot of mistakes, but he was a different driver on the last lap. He was spot on.[26]

Holden, though obviously disappointed, was magnanimous in defeat, offering praise for Klaffi:

> Fair play to him, we got a board + 6.4s at Ramsey on the last lap and I thought I had better go steady over the Mountain. I didn't make any mistakes, but he managed to get past me so he did well. We'd been struggling with speed all week so we put last year's engine in it. It was our last hope.[27]

For many observers the second sidecar race of 2010 was one of the all-time greats. At the end of the first lap Klaffenböck was over eight seconds behind Holden and then coming into the final lap he had dropped even further behind and was 10.15 seconds off. Yet on that final circuit he clawed it all back, and he took the win by 1.12 seconds – resulting in one of the closest ever sidecar finishes. Into the bargain he produced a lap over 114mph, which at that time was simply astonishing. Apart from the driver and passenger, no one was more pleased with that outcome that Padgetts Racing team boss Clive Padgett. The team had been heavily involved with supporting Klaffenböck's effort all week, and he had a Padgetts sticker on his fairing, so Clive didn't just win five races that week with Hutchy, as most people think, he actually won seven! The fact that an ex-World Champion, and a continental rider to boot, had come to the TT and had won was widely considered a great endorsement of the event. Dave Molyneux summed it up afterwards:

> For someone of his stature and his background to come here and win the TT is <u>massive</u>. I think the importance of it might still yet be underestimated. I look at him and think, 'Well done boy', because he has tried and tried and tried to succeed here. I think some people believe he didn't try hard enough at times but I can guarantee them that he did. He definitely tried hard enough, but at times it just didn't work for him. His only finishes have been brilliant ones, and his performances this year have been fantastic. It was a superb result. He bettered John Holden, Simon Neary, and Tim Reeves; these are fantastic drivers and teams. He bettered those guys and that was outstanding. That's why I wasn't disappointed this year, I made a mistake, I should have stuck with my practice set up and I didn't. I paid the price and I finished second. I think Patrick [Farrance] was disappointed because he firmly believed in my ability to overcome a deficit like that, but this is the way the TT is now. It's hard. It's competitive and it's hard. The standard in the sidecar class is extremely high. I might not be as fast as I used to be, in fact I know that I'm not, but I'm still

eager to win, and I have to work hard for that now ... Klaus Klaffenböck is a very successful businessman. He doesn't need to go racing to make a living, that's for sure. He's doing it because his heart is in it. It's in his family, a bit like the way it's in mine. One thing I do know about him is that he is an extremely determined man who will go to great lengths to achieve what he wants to achieve. He hit a stroke of luck when he got Dan Sayle on the side, because Dan is an absolutely outstanding passenger, one of the best of his generation. So they've got a great team together and I like that; I don't want an easy win, I want the hardest win I can possibly get, and if it means coming second or third sometimes then that's fine with me. At the end of the day they've got a great team together have those guys, and it's for me now to up my game, and I'm up for that.[28]

Klaffenböck returned to the TT in 2011 and with Dan Sayle in the chair again won the Sidecar A race, thus proving that the previous year's results were not a fluke. He did not, however, take part in the event again. Later he reflected on what had motivated him to come to the TT in the first place, and why he didn't continue to race on the Island:

Well, the aim always was to win the TT once. 2010 we won twice. And I thought, well, you have to come back one more time, to prove that it wasn't a one-off. So we won again 2011. And then it was done. The urge was gone. It definitely was the best thing I have ever done in my life. But also the most dangerous ... after we became world champions the pressure was gone. We did two more years, having been runner up in both seasons. And then we thought: What now? And the TT had always been on my mind. And we decided: Let's give it a try. Of course it was a new challenge for us. ... It takes special motorcycles for that race. The motorcycles we used for the world championship races cannot be used there. That was the first hurdle to overcome. And then we went there ... how shall I say ... a bit arrogant ... the World Champion is here and now we just do the race and get it done ... but the world looks very different once you are there. I can remember quite clearly. We started the first lap and after half the lap, around 30km, I thought 'we can't do it, I cannot do it. OK, let's go back to the pits, pack up and go home.' On the way back to the start/finish, I thought: 'Pack it up now? No, we can't do that. Let's try a second lap.' And from then on it went much better. And I must say, from the first lap on the IOM to the last I have become quicker every time. Each lap a little faster. And that way is how to do it there. It is a unique venue for racing. It is not like on a circuit ... if you just think of missing run-off zones etc. and because it is all long and fast you always have to keep the pace with your machine. It is a different way of driving compared to racing on short circuits.[29]

The 2011 Sidecar B Race went to John Holden, his first victory since arriving at the TT in 1988. It was a landmark moment for the competitor, who had been visiting the races since the 1960s and had watched Mike Hailwood win as a schoolboy with his parents. The win meant more to him than the considerable British Championship success that he had also enjoyed. However, despite the dedication of long-time competitors such as Holden, there were genuine concerns at this time that the sidecar class at the TT was not in a great position, because it was becoming far too expensive to compete there. Following the credit crunch and financial difficulties of 2008, the money was not around to back it. For various reasons, large corporate organisations did not want to back sidecars. The end result of this was that there were not enough young riders starting in the sport, and there were not enough riders staying in it, because there was not enough money around it for them to keep going. The TT and the people who ran it had to be given a lot of credit for being the last of the old school events in the world, and because they were prepared to help the riders to try to compete. They offered reasonable start money and they put up a decent prize fund, which was widely considered respectable and which reflected the endeavours and the risks of the crews. Most of those involved agreed that it would be good if competing could be made it easier, but the general feeling was that it was getting harder. The field might well have been getting stronger in terms of ability, but there was no question that it was also getting smaller.

Chapter 6

Age of the Champions

By the close of the first decade of the twenty-first century, in the currency of sidecar racing a win at the TT was worth more than the World Championship, and a number of riders who had been successful in the latter arena came to test themselves on the Mountain circuit. Indeed, such was the strength of the field by the end of the second decade that the TT was virtually a World Championship event of its own for sidecars.

As Formula 1 Sidecar World Champions, the Birchall brothers, Tom and Ben, who had made their British racing debut in 2004, made their first TT appearance in 2009 aboard an ex-Nick Crowe outfit that had been purchased for them by Dave Holden. For the Birchalls, TT was in their heart; as youngsters their father's passion had been motorcycle racing, and their summer holiday was the annual pilgrimage to the Isle of Man. Once again it was through the efforts of Paul Phillips and his team at the Motorsport Office – providing advice as well as practical assistance – that these up and coming talents were encouraged to come to the Island. The commitment and indeed almost obsession that they felt for the TT stemmed from childhood memories of watching Dave Saville and Rob Fisher from their camping site at Barregarrow, and for that matter also Dave Molyneux, for whom Ben Birchall would go on to become a mechanic. In the fickle world of sidecar racing, passenger swaps from year to year are common, but the almost unique aspect of two brothers racing together, as well as he longevity of their partnership, gave them a distinct advantage, as Ben observed:

> We take it for granted really, what an important factor that is, the fact that we're brothers and we've been together for our career in sidecar racing. Being brothers definitely helps because it's that sixth sense thing, he knows what I'm thinking before I've thought it a lot of the time! So when you put that on the bike, it works really well.[1]

After their initial appearance the brothers returned to World Championship racing, but in 2012 they joined Klaus Klaffenböck's Cofain Racing team for the Isle of Man TT. New rule changes put in place for the 2012 event outlawed expensive modifications and meant that outfits were now running virtually standard engines, in a bid to keep costs down. Despite a crash in practice they secured a respectable second and third places in the two races. The Birchalls had also suffered engine problems that had meant they were down on power, but the brothers were clearly delighted with their podium positions. Victory in both races that year, however, was to go to Kawasaki-powered Dave Molyneux and Patrick Farrance. For Molyneux, victory in Race 1 represented a particular achievement because it saw him become the only rider to have scored wins using all four Japanese engine manufacturers. It was his fifteenth TT win but it was the first for a clearly emotional Farrance, who stated that having started as a passenger aged 17, he had never dreamed of eventually winning a TT, and that it eclipsed his first World Championship win as a personal achievement. At the press conference afterwards Molyneux paid tribute to Farrance's drive and enthusiasm. He admitted that being so long at the TT meant that for him there was a danger of it becoming stale, but Farrance's hunger to win had rubbed off on him and given him renewed ambition.

Molyneux's main challenge came from Tim Reeves with Dan Sayle in the chair, but Reeves was beset with mechanical issues that restricted his performance. Despite a mechanic from Wilson Craig's racing team spending all day before the second race rebuilding an engine, and parts loaned or supplied by other solo teams in the paddock, Reeves never achieved the speed he felt he was capable of to challenge Molyneux. For the Manx driver by contrast it was a faultless TT with no mechanical issues and no moments of danger. The second race he regarded as one of the most enjoyable he had ever ridden in, and it gave him first place and win number sixteen to add to his tally.

Back with Klaffenböck for 2013, it was Ben and Tom Birchall who grabbed the early initiative in Sidecar Race 1. With ideal conditions all around the Mountain Course, they were leading at Glen Helen on the opening lap by 1.3 seconds from Tim Reeves and Dan Sayle of SMT Racing. Although they extended their lead to five seconds by Ramsey Hairpin, and to all intents and purposes victory was in the bag, Ben lost his line of sight for a second and clipped the bank at Creg ny Baa, putting them out of contention. That gave Tim and Dan a ten-second lead at the end of the lap and on the second circuit they continued to extend their advantage as they closed in on pre-race favourites Dave Molyneux/Patrick Farrance. Indeed, with Tim's best ever lap of the Mountain Course thus far, a speed of 114.608mph, they also took over the lead on the road, which gave them a twenty-second advantage over Molyneux/Farrance.

With the race now wrapped up, save for mechanical misfortune, Tim and Dan duly came home for a superb victory, their eventual winning margin over Conrad Harrison/Mike Aylott being 20.117 seconds, with Molyneux/Farrance nudged back to third. The victory gave both driver and team their first ever TT wins. For Sayle, it was his eighth TT win, making him the joint most successful passenger in the history of the event. Reeves became the first reigning Sidecar World Champion to win a TT race since Jock Taylor/Benga Johansson took victory in both legs back in 1981. Speaking afterwards, a delighted Tim said:

> I'm absolutely speechless and completely over the moon. You can't imagine how much it means to me to win today and as the reigning World Champion, it's even sweeter. Jock Taylor was my hero when I was growing up so to emulate him is something really special and apart from when my daughter Maisie was born, it's the best moment ever. On the first lap I was getting boards saying 'P1 +0' and then 'P2 +0' so I knew it was close but when I saw Dave just ahead of me, I couldn't believe it. As soon as I'd caught him on the road, I remembered what John McGuinness had said to me in terms of backing it off on the final lap and that's exactly what I did. Sidecar racing's

all about having the best team around you possible, so a massive thanks to Dan and all the sponsors, especially Robin Croft at SMT, the Haith's, H&S Contractors, Mark 'Brains' Woodage, the Padgetts and everyone else who's helped me. A big thanks as well to Gunther Reuschling, I'm sure he's listening in somewhere.[2]

Team owner Robin Croft added:

It's a dream come true and to think we only started speaking about this back in Macau last November. I could see the determination and desire in Tim that week so after a couple of glasses of wine, I said, 'Why don't we try and do it together?' And here we are seven months later with Tim having fulfilled his ambition and promise. Together with Dan, he did it in style and we're well, well pleased with the pair of them. It's been a difficult practice week and we've had our fair share of niggles but I think it was Joey Dunlop who said 'bad practice week, good race week' and that's what's happened so far. The whole team is thrilled and it's been a great start to race week for us.[3]

In the second race, the Birchalls scored their first TT win, something that was all the sweeter, coming as it did after the misfortune of the first outing. At the press conference afterwards, Ben Birchall was fulsome in his praise for Klaus Klaffenböck:

I just want to say a massive thanks to Klaus and his team, which is now our team, and we joined together, us and

Andy Mitchell, and joined Klaus last year, and it just brought us on, he saved me five or six years definitely and this week was tough. We didn't have much track time and you know he sat me down, he talked to me quite hard and said, 'You're not revving it enough, and you need to keep it flat out here and flat out there,' and I was like, 'That's easy for you to f***king say!' but you know he was right, and that's just … we unlocked it, we unlocked it in the first race, I made a mistake down to me, nobody else, and we just felt that we could carry it on into this one, and we did you know. Fair dues to Tom, I went just knocking three and four seconds off on each sector, and you know it's not easy for a passenger to suddenly speed up to that, with no warning and he did, he had to change his style and he did do, you know. Like, in that race out in the second lap I ran wide a few times, and I was pushing as hard as ever, and pushing too hard and I just reined it in, and I just caught sight of Dave and I thought, if I can just see him every now and again, and I wasn't sure what they were gonna do on the last lap. I know he's done it before, and I just held my pace as much as I could without doing too much, not too many revs in trying to bring it home, and we did do it. I must say thank you to everyone …[4]

In 2014, rule changes meant that it was possible once again for tuned engines to be used in the sidecar class. The regulations were now similar to those that had been in place in 2011 – the experiment in using stock motors in order to reduce costs had not proved successful, with research showing that it had produced no significant reduction in budgets for most teams. In contrast with the year previously, the 2014 TT races showed that there was still fight left in the Old Guard! Sidecar Race 1 went to Conrad Harrison, a veteran racer who made his first appearance back in 1993, while Race 2 was taken by Dave Molyneux, with passenger Patrick Farrance. In lap one of the opening Sure Sidecar race of TT 2014, at Glen Helen, Ben and Tom Birchall led John Holden/Andrew Winkle by 0.7 second with Dave Molyneux/Patrick Farrance not far behind in third place. As lap one went on, the Birchall brothers – competing again for Klaus Klaffenböck's Cofain Racing team – stretched out a reasonable lead over John Holden and Dave Molyneux. By the end of the first lap the Birchalls led by over four seconds as Molyneux/Farrance and Holden/Winkle headed the chasing pack, the two crews battling over second place.

On lap two, however, there was drama as the Birchall brothers were involved in a crash at Black Dub. This meant that Dave Molyneux was now leading the race by ten seconds over nearest challenger John Holden. Conrad Harrison had moved into third position, while Tim Reeves moved up to fourth place on his SMT Racing-backed outfit. Molyneux's lead over Holden grew on lap two as the sixteen-time TT winner was giving it everything he had in order to secure another famous win on his DMR Kawasaki outfit.

The final lap of the race beckoned, with Molyneux's lead over Holden a big one, with Harrison not far behind the 2011 Sidecar TT Race 2 winner. Tim Reeves held fourth position, with Ian Bell on his TT comeback proving that he could still mix it at the front in sidecar races at Isle of Man TT by holding a top five placing.

Lap three initially saw Dave Molyneux/Patrick Farrance continue to build up their advantage out at the front but then mechanical issues struck their outfit. They were suddenly out of the race, which meant now Conrad Harrison/Mike Aylott had hit the front by 0.9 second over John Holden/Andrew Winkle. From here Harrison made no mistakes to cross the line as winner at the end of lap three, recording a popular and well-deserved first TT victory. The modest Yorkshireman commented afterwards:

> You don't win a TT for yourself, you win it for your team, you win it for everybody – everybody shares it ... You just share it, everybody is out there, everybody is clapping and cheering you on ... I was lucky this year with a little bit of sponsorship from Printer Roller Services because the engines are a lot more money this year with it being open rules, and I've been lucky there ... [In the race] I saw 'P2 1' and I thought 'there's something wrong here! Has somebody put the wrong pitboard out?' I was lucky with the run that I got, because Tim [Reeves] dragged me on, and I could see John [Holden] in front, and it does drag you on a bit if you can see the other person in front. At 114 that's the fastest lap I've ever done.[5]

In Race 2 the dice tumbled the other way and Kawasaki-powered Molyneux benefited from the technical difficulties of others. The leader at Glen Helen on lap one was John Holden with Andrew Winkle, who established a two-second lead over Conrad Harrison and Mike Aylott. Molyneux and Farrance occupied third place, while Tim Reeves and Gregory Cluze completed the top four. Holden and Winkle's lead over Harrison and Aylott grew as the Silicone Engineering Racing Honda-powered outfit was flying and the pair looked to have a great chance of a second TT victory. Reeves and Cluze were showing good pace on the SMT Racing-backed outfit. Karl Bennett and Lee Cain were impressive in holding a top six position as lap one entered its final stages.

Holden and Winkle's lead at end of lap one was more than seventeen seconds over Molyneux and Farrance. The latter had edged in front of Harrison and Aylott, who now held third place. Further down the field, Alan Founds and Tom Peters showed themselves to be potential stars of the future by holding eighth position as the race entered lap two. By now Holden and Winkle had a commanding lead over Molyneux/Farrance, and by Glen Helen the gap had risen to eighteen seconds. Harrison/Aylott maintained third place on the Printing Roller Services-backed outfit. Ian and Carl Bell were in a great battle with Karl Bennett and Lee Cain as both outfits fought for fifth place. Holden/Winkle's lead over Molyneux/Farrance had now come down to around fifteen seconds, and multiple TT winner Molyneux was clearly on a charge as he looked set on mounting a challenge for what would be his second Kawasaki-powered TT triumph.

By the end of lap two Holden/Winkle's lead over Molyneux/Farrance had been cut to eleven seconds, Corad Harrison/Aylott remained in third place, and Reeves/Cluze were secure in fourth place in front of Bennett/Cain.

Mechanical issues forced Ian Bell/Carl Bell out of the race at the end of lap two, and soon technical problems were to hit Holden/Winkle's outfit – the duo's lead was down to only three seconds at Glen Helen as Molyneux/Farrance could sense victory was within their grasp.

By Ballaugh Bridge Molyneux/Farrance had a more than fifteen-second lead over Holden/Winkle, who despite suffering technical issues were determined to carry on even if only touring, Holden later telling journalists that he would have considered tenth place better than nothing. Conrad Harrison/Mike Aylott were now not far behind challenging for second place. The rest of the final lap of the race saw Molyneux/Farrance maintaining a brisk pace and extending their lead out in front. As they did so Harrison/Aylott had moved into second place by Ramsey on lap three, in front of Holden/Winkle. Across the line went Molyneux and Farrance to take Sure Sidecar TT Race 2 victory. Farrance told the press conference afterwards:

> It really is the best feeling in the world. That circuit out there is the best thrill that anybody could do; to be able to do that, what we do out there it's unbelievable, and to be riding alongside Dave is just fantastic ... To come away with a win, it really is brilliant.[6]

Molyneux, meanwhile, was philosophical:

> I really made work for everybody [between the two races] – just electrical issues ... It's an Achilles Heel of a sidecar, they just bring up the worst of racing really, but we went back to a kit ECU which is like a basic system and Dave

Hagen spent till midnight last night mapping the thing in, and it was just suck it and see and make the best of it, and it would have gone another three laps I'm quite sure, only for the fuel; we ran out of fuel round Brandish on the last lap – I was like swishing it around and turning the ignition on and off – it banged into life and went, but anyway it was OK – eventful! We hit two rabbits, a bird and had a scare at Greeba. Going into Greeba Castle … going round the left-hander coming into Greeba Castle it's a flat-out kink, and then right at the last minute, probably only 50 or 60 metres to go, you just flick two gears down and go through the section – [well] I could only get one gear and I ran wide on the left, pulled it in, got in a drift, left the ground over the right-hander, bumped into the blinkin' air bags, and it just snaked us off down the road.[7]

Luckily Farrance was unshaken by the incident and the duo went on to take the win. This victory was Dave's seventeenth overall on the Mountain Course, and it was Patrick Farrance's third time as a victor at the TT. Conrad Harrison/Mike Aylott finished in second place over forty seconds down, but the runner-up placed finish meant overall TT 2014 sidecar championship victory for the duo.

Sidecar Race 2 at the 2015 TT would further underline the fact that the Old Guard was not going to hand over control without putting up a fight! Despite the Birchalls having a lead of 7.5 seconds after two laps of the race, an amazing final lap by Dave Molyneux (passengered by relative novice Ben Binns) saw them break the longest standing of the Mountain Course lap records at that time. Their exhilarating speed of 116.785mph saw Molyneux and Binns overhaul Nick Crowe and Dan Sayle's lap record of 115.667mph, which had stood since the 2007 TT, and although the Birchalls upped their pace and took victory, also breaking the old lap record in the process, they were still marginally outside the Molyneux/Binns time. In what became the fastest sidecar race in TT history up to that time, third-placed crew John Holden and Dan Sayle also lapped at more than 116mph. Molyneux said afterwards:

> I tried as hard as I could and as hard as I dare. I screwed up a few lines. It got very hot under the fairing and my gloves rode up a bit. I've got to give Nick Crowe credit for holding on to the record for so long. Nick really did something special that day back in 2007.[8]

The achievement was all the more remarkable given that it was only Binns' third TT outing, but Molyneux went on:

> There were a lot of doubters out there, saying that he had only lapped at 105mph. Well, 105mph is not slow and I knew he could do it. I pushed him really hard. He is well suited to the way I ride.[9]

The Birchalls, meanwhile, had developed a relationship with frame manufacturer Louis Christian while riding for Klaus Klaffenböck's team, and when they decided to branch out on their own approached Christian for a new outfit. However, to their dismay the constructor announced that he had ceased producing Formula 2 chassis, but, he added that he had some unused parts available and invited Ben to Switzerland to see what he had to offer. With Tom Birchall's welding skills coming in useful, the duo spent three months in Switzerland constructing their outfit. So impressed was Christian with their skills that he eventually allowed them to build two other machines, which they sold to cover the cost of their own. It incorporated numerous ideas, for example differences in gear change and fuel tank, that the Birchalls had developed over previous TT races. Further refinements in terms of radiator position and bodywork style would come, leading each year to greater and greater speed. For the first time, as well as developing a seat tailored to the physique of the driver, they applied the same principle to the passenger platform, shaping it to suit Tom. The development allowed for more fluid movement of the passenger, further enhancing speed.

The first outing aboard the self-built outfit was in 2016 and, despite the hurdles they faced in assembling and financing their own team, they led the first race by a commanding more than twenty seconds. Fate intervened, however, and despite long thousands spent in tuning the engine, a 48 pence bolt snapped, leaving them coasting to a halt. They drowned their sorrows in the Sulby Glen Hotel, as victory went to John Holden and Andy Winkle. However, the disappointment only served to fuel the Birchalls' determination in Race 2, which they won ahead of Holden and Winkle, and Tim Reeves and Patrick Farrance. Despite the wet conditions in 2017, the Birchalls set a new lap record, and in fact were the only race team at the event to achieve this. With almost perfect weather in 2018, however, and an outfit that had been refined year on year, the brothers were set to take the sidecar lap record into a new dimension. After a difficult Practice Week, while not exactly entering Race 1 blind, the brothers were not as prepared for it as they might have been. Ben admitted that on lap one he had almost put the machine into Braddan churchyard, but with a red flag incident, and later a restart, he explained that he had cleared his head a little and produced three laps all inside the existing lap record, to beat John Holden and Lee Cain (second) and Tim Reeves and Mark Wilks (third):

> It's not easy, is it. None of it's easy ... We caught a couple of birds, had a couple of bird strikes ... But the track is in mint condition, the rubber is down, it's a good temperature really, I sort of like it that temperature, not too hot, tarmac's not too hot and it was working really well. You never know what pace you can run around here, or I don't, I just try to hit all the right bits and keep pushing on as smooth as we can. Obviously Tom's incredible, you know, doing a job like that. It was great, faultless really, we just had a bit of a moment at Windy Corner, I think wind got it a bit – that's what I'm blaming it on anyway! Other than that it was fantastic. Chris builds us some incredible engines and we have a great team that year on year keep digging in and doing it for us and helping us to be here.[10]

Race 2 produced the same line-up on the podium, in the same order, but that scarcely began to tell the tale of what had just happened. Commentators at the time stated that the lap record had not merely been broken, but obliterated. The first sub-nineteen-minute sidecar lap had been achieved, thirteen years after Dave Molyneux had broken the twenty-minute barrier. Questioned afterwards if the fine weather had been the decisive factor, Ben indicated that it had played a part, but only in as much as it allowed rivals Reeves and Holden to improve their times, thus pushing him harder. He credited the achievement more to brother Ben, who had taken a new approach to some bends and corners in an effort to wring even greater grip and therefore speed from the outfit. He added:

> I saw minus 2 [on a board], I thought, 'Aagh! That's no good' so we pushed on, I thought, 'Yeah, it's time to go' – I've pulled the pin as hard as I can. Obviously Tom was with me every step of the way, and it's just incredible. I did go out to do that, I just went to go as clean and as hard as we could, and we got rewarded with a fantastic lap time and a fantastic win. To do the double, I think it's a double double, I think that's great, I really like that.[11]

He conceded that the faster pace meant he wasn't always as neat with his lines as he hoped and went into some corners deeper than he should have, but the only real 'moment' was at Ballaugh went he nearly went into the Raven pub! His brother Tom added:

> It was just something else … I saw a board myself and never really looked but I thought, 'Something's gonna have to happen now' … And then we got out of Quarter Bridge so well it was like a rocket going up to Braddan

and I thought, 'Right, something'll happen here now,' and sure enough it did, and it was awesome, an awesome lap, and a real pleasure to be part of it. It was tough, don't get me wrong, but smooth and fast and just what you'd expect from the TT course. It was awesome, I loved it.[12]

For the Birchalls, the attraction of the TT was its unpredictability. Even with their track record, the brothers never regarded a win as a done deal and still had to work hard for everything.

While no longer attracting the German and Swiss legions of the 1960s, the TT still draws in dedicated foreign riders. In recent years, one very important factor has been the consistently high number of entries from France. For over twenty years the TT has been the main focus for a number of French teams as the rigours of the Mountain Course and the challenge of completing races lasting over an hour, have in turn, improved the quality of F2 sidecar racing in the French Championships. One could be forgiven for thinking it would be the Swiss LCR construction that would dominate, but the French have usually used British chassis such as Shelbourne, Ireson, Windle, Bellas and most often (Tony) Baker. That is until 2013. Step forward Sam Gache. Sole constructor of the SGR, he provided the outfit that would see the debut at the TT of Estelle Leblond. She had won the French Championship with Thomas Quintre the previous year, but for her first Isle of Man appearance in 2013 enlisted the help of the experienced Sebastien Lavorel. They finished both races in twenty-ninth place, lapped at over 101mph and consequently Leblond emulated her mother Sylvie, also a sidecar racer, in being awarded the Susan Jenness Trophy, in 2014. This award is presented by the TT Supporters' Club to the female competitor who has made the most meritorious performance in the previous year. In 2015 Leblond was awarded the trophy for the second time, having achieved a personal best at the previous year's TT in Race 2. With passenger Melanie Farnier, she holds the record as the fastest all-female sidecar crew at the TT.

In 2017 there were also some outstanding performances at the TT by other female sidecar competitors; Fiona Baker-Holden, accompanying dad, Tony, had a great TT, gaining two bronze replicas for eighth and sixth places with average race speeds well in excess of 109mph. Chrissie Clancy, as passenger to Mick Alton and in only her second TT, achieved her fastest ever lap in Race 2, 108.785mph; this resulted in an eleventh place and a bronze replica, something she had already secured with twelfth in the first outing for sidecars. It was a similar story for Julie Canipa, who, after acting as ballast for Doug Chandler at the TTs of 2015 and 2016, admirably assisted veteran driver Greg Lambert to eighth and fourteenth positions, taking home two bronze replicas. Beset by various problems during the fortnight, local sidecar driver Debbie Barron regrouped, pulling all her resources together to complete the distance in the second of her events at an average of speed 94.406mph.

Other stalwarts of the TT paddock include the Founds brothers, Pete and Alan, who in contrast with the Birchalls race against each other rather than together. The sons of TT racer Des Founds, the pair spent many of their childhood holidays at racing circuits and paddocks. Pete made his Mountain Course debut in 1997, and Alan arrived in 2005. Alan commented:

The noise, the banter, the smells, the antics and the stories that you just couldn't make up. The camaraderie between teams was something special and it taught us all an invaluable lesson in life when it comes to 'love thy neighbour'. There wasn't anything that wouldn't be loaned or borrowed to your closest rival, that's just how it was ... Myself and Pete, as the only Founds to be currently racing at the TT, share a similar outlook on the TT fortnight and one which is heavily influenced by our childhood. It's fair to say that we are both very committed to one day standing on the top step of the TT podium and for myself, getting to where my dad never did, knowing how hard he tried and the sacrifices he made, is an amazing challenge. This year is my 5th year competing at the TT and it will be Pete's 3rd. Close in brotherly love as we are, we definitely want to beat each other on or off the track in most competitions and there is no love lost when we do![13]

Brother Pete added:

Obviously for me the plan is to win a TT. We both know it's possible for one of us to win it, but all the cherries need to line up and, as you say, on our limited budget our engines will need to be exemplary. If I won one, I feel like this would close the circle for me, but then I thought the same about winning a British Championship and here I am again, competing for a third title. In reality, I'm not sure! I guess it depends on how I'm feeling and what else is going on in my life at the time, after all it does take some commitment. I'll probably look at another sidecar challenge.[14]

After a two-year lay-off in 2020 and 2021, the TT returned with a roar in 2022. The enforced period of absence had given sidecar teams the opportunity to experiment with different approaches and try out new ideas. Dave Molyneux, after an entire career on Japanese machinery, was back, but this time on KTM engines. One of the attractions of the Austrian manufacturer's motors – aside from their already proven power – was the fact that they would fit a sidecar chassis without the expensive modifications (such as removal and shortening on the sump) that many other engines required.

Despite being one of the stalwarts of the sidecar class, and also one of its greatest advocates, Molyneux found himself losing his passion for racing as a result of ageing regulations that had stipulated the use of a 600cc four-cylinder engine since 1991.

With parts becoming increasingly scarce and costs soaring as a result, Molyneux successfully convinced the event organisers to adopt a fresh set of technical regulations capped at 900cc twin-cylinders. With Daryl Gibson in the chair, Molyneux had already found that fitting a KTM-manufactured 890cc twin in his DMR machine was enabling him to lap quicker than ever:

> We've been riding since 1990 a 600cc, four-cylinder, four-stroke and never in the history of the sport has there been a category of engine use that has lasted so long. It is great for the sport, but everything has its time and for me, in 2018, I was seeing a little bit of a crack in the job and we

were struggling to get engines. We depend on breaking yards, salvage yards to get a supply and trying to get a 600cc engine right now is really difficult and because they are in short supply, price goes up. Back then in 2018, I thought we had to introduce something as an alternative and we need youths coming in, not old-timers like me. I had to put my money where my mouth is and get this 900cc, twin-cylinder thing going, so running the 890cc KTM is really wonderful. I think I would have quit if I'd have continued with the 600[cc]. This is a breath of fresh air and I am enjoying riding it.

It has given me a new lease of life for the short term, I have not enjoyed my racing so much. I can't even remember the last time I enjoyed it so much and I'm equalling my personal bests at every track I go to. I feel like I can go to the TT and be competitive.[15]

In the winter 2017 edition of the TT Supporters' Club magazine, Isle of Man Government Department of Economic Development Motorsport Manager Paul Philips was asked about the decline in entries for the sidecar races at the TT in recent years. His answer was frank and addressed the major issues facing the class:

> There has been a general decline in sidecar racing across the world for more than a decade and the TT is not immune to that. I worry about the future of sidecar racing at the TT because of the age profile of the competitors and the issues around the future supply of 600cc engines, which are becoming more and more obsolete as the motorcycle

manufacturers, one by one, pull out of that market. That said, the sidecar class at the TT remains important to us as promoters and popular with the fans. We are proud to have what are undoubtedly the most competitive and most high-profile sidecar races in the world with global TV coverage along with some exciting new names – the Founds brothers and Lewis Blackstock for example – coming to the fore; this bodes well for the future.[16]

The sidecar class newcomer has traditionally been of an older average age than that of a solo debutant, largely due to the higher initial costs of acquiring and setting up an outfit, but if the issue of increasing costs associated with the sport can be addressed by moves such as that advocated by Molyneux, then this in turn should encourage a younger class of competitor. At the 2022 TT the most exciting development was arguably the exhilarating performance of a new brother-brother pairing, that of Ryan and Callum Crowe, the sons of five-time TT winner Nick Crowe. Having the made their debut in 2019, when they recorded the fastest ever lap by a newcomer at 113.53mph, the duo were raring to go. At the start of Practice Week Ryan commented:

It's been a bit of a wake-up call when you go back down Bray Hill I suppose, we had a bit of a fuel problem on Sunday night ... I feel very confident in what we're doing. Obviously we're testing a new bike, its brand new, we only just picked it up from Ben and Tom Birchall about four weeks ago. We did a couple of short circuits on it, just testing. It's all been good but it's only here where you find your faults really I suppose, but it's been good. I'm enjoying the bike, I like the way it rides, it's fast, it's good, Callum's good we're all good to go … I just want to finish the race to be honest, to beat my personal best from last time. I think we've got a bit to go, to stretch our legs and just pick up the pace gradually. I went out on Sunday just to have a shake down, I wasn't anywhere near flat out. We had a few problems, broke down at Kirk Michael, but it was steady away to Kirk Michael and it was still averaging 110, so it was a good pace for a first night lap on a brand new bike.[17]

His brother Callum added:

I'm a bit more nervous than in in 2019 because I know the speed we did then and everyone asks, 'Are you going to go even faster,' and yeah, that comes along with the racing, but I definitely feel like it's more bumpy than in 2019. I think that's maybe because we've been away from it for so long. Paul Richards from Maxton has got his work cut out here, were trying to work alongside him now getting comfy in the bike.[18]

Despite their modest expectations they bettered this by some margin in achieving second place in the 2022 Race 1 event. Victory across the board, however, went to the Birchall brothers, whose performance was growing more assured year on year, and whose grip on the sidecar TT races seemed ever tighter.

Epilogue – The Future

Where does the sidecar class at the Isle of Man TT go in the next 100 years? The obvious question has to be asked: how much longer can we expect to see the event run on carbon-based fuels? The TT Zero race was dropped from the schedule in 2022 due to pressure of time on the roads, but to many observers with the UK committed to ending petrol and diesel engine production by the 2030s, electric propulsion has to be the way forward in one form or another.

Will the sidecar TT embrace electric power, or will it remain wedded to high-octane petrol, as some form of classic race for the machinery of yesteryear? No doubt this would have an appeal to many, as classic racing is unquestionably popular with thousands of fans, but in a way this would be a betrayal of what the sidecar TT has always been about. Far more than solo racing, the sidecar event has attracted the innovators, the engineers, and the mechanics who think outside of the box. To fossilise it in the amber of late-twentieth century technology would surely crush any incentive to innovate or improve, and would widen further the gap between sidecars and the mainstream motorcycle manufacturers.

On the face of it, current electric motorcycle power plants are unsuitable for sidecars. The battery units are their Achilles heel, due to their weight and bulk. Hydrogen technology is also under development in the UK as an alternative to battery power, but with the gas being even more volatile than petrol, it requires an altogether stronger fuel tank to contain it, and using it safely in a racing machine would pose challenges, as anyone who has seen footage of the *Hindenburg* disaster will know …

Critics might also point to the fact that electric-powered machines are currently considerably slower than their petrol-driven counterparts, but with ever-increasing speeds at the TT once again becoming a concern among some observers, would an initial reduction of perhaps 10mph in lap speeds be such a bad thing? We might well be back where we started in less than ten years.

Notes

Chapter 1

1. *TT Special*, 7 June 1948, p.13.
2. Op cit.
3. Op cit.
4. *Isle of Man Times*, 16 June 1923.
5. *Isle of Man Examiner*, 19 June 1925.
6. *Motorcycle Sport*, September 1986, p.422.
7. *Sport* [Dublin], 12 December 1925.
8. *Leeds Mercury*, 6 December 1927.

Chapter 2

1. Stan Dibben, interview with author.
2. *The Classic Motorcycle*, 29 November 2012.
3. Dibben, interview with author.
4. Op cit.
5. *Classic Motorcycling Legends*, No. 11, 1990, p.6.
6. *Cycle World*, 1 January 1967.
7. *Isle of Man Times*, 7 June 1957.
8. *Motor Cycling*, 27 June 1957, p.272.
9. *TT Special*, 3 June 1959.
10. John Chisnall and Anthony Davis, *And the Wheels Went Round*, Wivenhoe, 2019, p.38.
11. Op cit, p.69.
12. Op cit, p.60.
13. *Classic Motorcycle*, 30 November 2012.

14. Op cit.
15. Op cit.
16. Op cit.

Chapter 3

1. Dibben, interview with author.
2. Max Deubel, interview with author.
3. Op cit.
4. Op cit.
5. Lothar Mildebrath *Münchener Meistermacher Maschinen* Stassfurt, 2013, p.7.
6. Duke Video, *Best of British: BSA*, author's transcript.
7. Karl Schleuter, letter to author, 20 January 2018.
8. Colin Seeley, *Racer – and the Rest!*, Gateshead, 2007, p.74.
9. Op cit, p.75.
10. *Motor Cycle News*, 12 June 1963, p.6.
11. *Motor Cycle News*, 19 June 1963, p.8.
12. *TT News*, 5 June 2010, p.7.
13. *TT News*, 2016 No. 3, p.8.
14. *Classic Racer*, May 2019, p.54.
15. *TT News*, 2016, No. 3, p.9.
16. Seeley, p.183.
17. Chisnall and Davis, p.72.
18. *TT News*, 2017, No. 2, p.29.
19. *Motorcycle Sport* January 1969, p.28.
20. *TT News*, 2016, No. 3, p.9.
21. Interview with Elizabeth Marin www.ttsupporterrsclub.com
22. Op cit.
23. *Rocinante Mecanico* newsletter, 28 April 2012.
24. www.motorcycletimeline.com
25. Op cit.
26. *Motorcycle Weekly*, 9 June 1973, p.8.

27. *TT Special*, 4 June 1973, p.14.
28. *Motorcycle Sport*, September 1976.
29. Op cit.

Chapter 4

1. Kenny Arthur, interview with author.
2. George O'Dell and Ian Beacham, *Sidecar Championship*, London, 1978, p.81.
3. Op cit, p.82.
4. Arthur, interview with author.
5. Op cit.
6. O'Dell, p.86.
7. www.dickgreasley.com
8. www.wemoto.be/news/article/993/motorcycle_hero_rolf_biland
9. www.stevesplace.org
10. www.bonhams.com
11. *Motorcycle Racing*, June 1979, p.17.
12. *Motor Cycle News*, 10 June 1981.
13. *Motor Cycle News*, 10 June 1981.
14. *Motorcycle Sport*, October 1981, p.519.
15. Op cit, p.520.
16. *Motor Cycle News*, 9 February 2016.
17. *Classic Racer*, 13 February 2018.
18. *Fingal Independent*, 23 May 2020.
19. TT Programme, 1985, p.49.
20. Op cit, p.47.
21. Op cit, p.49.
22. Op cit, p.49.
23. TT Programme 1990, p.19.
24. www.ttwebsite.com
25. Dave Molyneux, *The Racer's Edge*, Barnsley, 2011, p.32.

26. TT Programme 1991, p.82.
27. Op cit, p.92.
28. Op cit, p.80.
29. Op cit p.81.
30. *Classic Racer*, April 2019, p.60.
31. Molyneux, p.45.
32. *Island Racer*, 2004 p.83.
33. *Classic Racer*, May/June 2021, p.84.
34. Molyneux, p.59.
35. Op cit, p.67.
36. Op cit, p.69.
37. Op cit, p.71.
38. www.ttwebsite.com
39. 3-Wheeling, *1997 Sidecar TT* documentary, author's transcript.
40. Molyneux, p.82.
41. Op cit, p.84.
42. Op cit, p.84.
43. *Motor Cycle News*, 7 June 2000, p.50.
44. Op cit.
45. Molyneux, p.90.
46. Op cit, p.94.

Chapter 5

1. *Motor Cycle News*, 16 June 2004, p.58.
2. Molyneux, p.96.
3. Op cit, p.99.
4. Op cit, p.100.
5. Op cit, p.102.
6. *TT News*, 8 June 2006, p.9.
7. Op cit.
8. *TT News*, 8 June 2006, p.18.
9. *Classic Racer*, 13 February 2018.

10. Molyneux, p.109.
11. Op cit, p.110.
12. Op cit, p.111.
13. Op cit, p.116.
14. TT Programme 2008, p.60.
15. Op cit, p.51.
16. Molyneux, p.119.
17. *Motor Cycle News*, 6 June 2008.
18. Op cit.
19. TT Programme 2009, p.80.
20. Molyneux, p.121.
21. Op cit, p.122.
22. Op cit, p.124.
23. *TT News* Race Edition One, 5 June 2010, p.20.
24. Op cit.
25. *TT News* Race Edition Two, 10 June 2010, p.17.
26. Op cit, p.18.
27. Op cit.
28. Molyneux, p.127.
29. *Klaffi in Schwanenstadt* interview, 11 September 2014, author's transcript.

Chapter 6

1. Ben Birchall, interview with author.
2. www.isleofman.com
3. Op cit.
4. Ben Birchall, 2013 Sidecar TT Race 2 press conference, author's transcript.
5. Conrad Harrison, 2014 Sidecar TT Race 1 press conference, author's transcript.
6. Patrick Farrance, 2014 Sidecar TT Race 2 press conference, author's transcript.

7. Dave Molyneux, 2014 Sidecar TT Race 2 press conference, author's transcript.
8. *TT News*, 2015, No. 3, p.22.
9. *TT News*, 2015, No. 3, p.22.
10. Ben Birchall, 2018 Sidecar TT Race 1 press conference, author's transcript.
11. Ben Birchall, 2018 Sidecar TT Race 2 press conference, author's transcript.
12. Tom Birchall, 2018 Sidecar TT Race 2 press conference, author's transcript.
13. *TT Supporters Club Magazine*, Summer 2018.
14. Op cit.
15. www.bennetts.co.uk
16. *TT supporters club Magazine*, Winter 2017.
17. Isle of Man TV interview, author's transcript.
18. Op cit.

Bibliography

Allen, C.E., 'The Legendary Sidecar Races of 1923-24-25' in *Motorcycle Sport*, September 1986, p.421

Allen, C.E., 'Something For Nothing?' in *Motorcycle Sport*, September 1988, p.48

Bye, George, 'My Second Drive in the Sidecar TT' in *Motorcycle Sport*, January 1969, p.26

Chisnall, John and Davis, Anthony, *And the Wheels Went Round*, Wivenhoe, 2019

'D.S.', 'Race Diary – The Story of a Sidecar TT entry' in *Motorcycle Sport*, October 1981, p.518

Mildebrath, Lothar, *Münchener Meistermacher Maschinen*, Stassfurt, 2013

Mitchinson, Milton A., 'Look ... No Hands! Experiences of a Sidecar TT Passenger' in *Motorcycle Sport*, September 1976, p.354

Molyneux, Dave, *The Racer's Edge*, Barnsley, 2011

O'Dell, George and Beacham, Ian, *Sidecar Championship*, London, 1978

Richardson, Matthew, *TT Titans*, Barnsley, 2018

Seeley, Colin, *Racer ... And the Rest*, Volume 1, Gateshead, 2007

Index

Abbott, Steve, 104, 107, 109
Armstrong, Brian, 47
Arnold, Rose, 64–6
Arthur, Kenny, 84, 86–92, 98
Attenberger, Johann, 22
Auerbacher, Georg, 22, 27, 45, 47, 51, 53, 57, 60–2, 68, 69
Australia, 26, 35, 78
Auto Cycle Union, 12–13, 15–16, 19, 26, 30, 53, 58, 67, 89, 96, 114–15, 126, 129, 142
Aylott, Mike, 189–92

BMW motors, 21–4, 27, 28, 35–7, 39, 43, 45–6, 48–50, 55–6, 58, 61–2, 64, 66, 68–72, 74–5, 81
BSA motors, 44–5, 54–5, 64, 75–6, 82, 97
Ballacraine, 47, 57, 74, 133, 149
Ballaugh, 66, 74, 87, 90, 93, 103, 116, 166, 170–1, 191, 196
Barker, Tony, 107
Bass, Anthony 'Slick', 126–7, 130–1, 142
Beeton, Jack, 35–6

Beevers, Bill, 32–6
Bell, Carl, 190–1
Bell, Geoff, 119
Bell, Ian, 119, 138–40, 142, 188, 190–1
Bennett, Alec, 3
Bennett, Karl, 190
Biggs, Philip, 133
Biggs, Vince, 104, 132
Biland, Rolf, 93–5, 97
Bingham, Dennis & Julia, 104, 107–109
Binns, Ben, 192–3
Birch, Allan, 47–50
Birch, Kenny, 96
Birchall, Ben, 182–4, 186, 188, 192–6, 202
Birchall, Tom, 182, 184, 186, 188, 192–7, 202
Bird, Colin, 66
Birks, Chas, 106
Blacklock, Ken, 79–81
Bliss, Eric, 23, 25–6, 44
Boddice, Bill, 21, 26–7, 30, 47, 54

Boddice, Mick, 54–5, 75–6, 97, 101, 103, 106, 111–12, 118–20, 127, 133, 140, 154
Braddan Bridge, 8, 45, 94
Brandish, 28, 31–2, 42, 44, 91, 192
Bregazzi, Eric, 112
Bridcutt, Owen, 11
Brown, Peter, 67
Bullock, Martin, 144
Burghardt, Horst, 45
Burns, Mick, 81, 86
Burton, Lowry, 107
Busch, Dieter, 68, 70–1
Bye, George, 60, 62–3

Cain, Lee, 190, 195
Camathias, Florian, 22, 28, 32, 35, 40–2, 45, 47–8, 50–2, 55
Campbell, Alex, 78
Campbell, Ray, 37
Cannell, Geoff, 113
Carpenter, Neil, 140
Chisnall, John, 33–6
Christian, Louis, 193, 194
Cluze, Gregory, 190
Clypse Course, 16, 21, 23, 25–6, 28, 30–4, 38
Copson, Bill, 66
Cox, Mark, 164, 166, 168–71, 173
Craig, Joe, 20
Croft, Robin, 186

Cron, Fritz, 22, 24
Crowe, Callum, 202–203
Crowe, Nick, 145–6, 152–4, 158, 160–1, 163–4, 166–70, 173, 182, 193, 202
Crowe, Ryan, 202–203
Cushnahan, Pat, 107

Davies, Mark, 151
Davis, Tony, 58
Denny, Walter, 7–8
Deubel, Max, 22, 39–43, 47, 51–3
Dibben, Stan, 17–18, 20, 25, 29, 38–9
Dixon, Frederick William, 2–8, 10, 14, 41, 58
Douglas motorcycles, 2–4, 10
Drion, Jacques, 18–19, 22, 29
Duke, Geoff, 40
Dunelt & Elliots motorcycles, 11
Dungworth, Barry, 47

Eden, R.G., 24
Ellison, Karl, 118, 121
Enders, Klaus, 58, 68–74
Engelhardt, Ralph, 58, 70, 72–3
Excelsior motorcycles, 15

Faragher, Andy, 153, 164, 168
Farnier, Melanie, 198
Farrance, Patrick, 175, 178, 183–5, 188–92, 194

Fath, Helmut, 40–1, 55–7, 61, 68
Faust, Willy, 23
First World War, 1–2
Fisher, Rob, 122–4, 127, 132–3, 135–6, 138–41, 182
Forest, Jack, 35
Founds, Alan, 190, 198–9, 202
Founds, Pete, 198–9, 202
Freeman, Charlie, 28, 33, 35

Gibson, Daryl, 200
Gilera motors, 19, 51, 55
Greasley, Dick, 80, 89–92, 103
Greeba, 81, 192
Grinton, George, 10–11
Grunwald, Manfred, 29

Hagen, Dave, 148, 192
Hailwood, Mike, 41, 42
Hallam, Craig, 123, 136, 147–8, 150
Hancock, Dave, 151
Hanks, Norman, 59, 63–6, 132
Hanks, Roy, 53–4, 56, 63–6, 104, 106, 109, 111–12, 132–3, 152–4
Hanks, Tom, 109, 110–11
Hardman, Colin, 140–41
Harris, Peter 'Pip', 19–20, 22, 24, 27, 35–7, 40, 47, 52
Harrison, Conrad, 188–92

Harrison, Terry, 35
Hawes, Dick, 94
Herzig, Alfred, 48
Heukerott, Gert, 75
Hill, Peter, 125, 127–30
Hillberry, 8, 31–2, 66, 91, 117
Hillebrand, Fritz, 20, 28–9
Hobson, Mac, 79, 81, 86, 96–7
Hoehler, Horst, 40–1
Hoerner, Emil, 41, 47
Holden, Fred, 54
Holden, John, 138, 152–3, 159, 166, 176–8, 180–1, 188–91, 193–6
Holder, Graham, 21
Honda motors, *xi*, 114, 118–20, 127, 133–9, 141, 144, 148, 152–3, 156, 159, 162, 164, 167, 175, 190
Hope, Darren, 146, 152–3
Hughes, Geoff, 61
Hughes Brothers sidecars, 7
Humby, Graham, 28

Indian motorcycles, 2
Ireson, Trevor, 103, 114, 197
Isle of Man Examiner, 11
Isle of Man Times, 9

Jewell, Doug, 134–5
Johansson, Bengt-Goran (Benga), 99–101, 104–105

KTM motors, 200
Kawasaki, 75, 101, 114–15, 118, 173–5, 183, 188–90
Kalauch, Wolfgang, 53, 89
Kinley, Chris, 146
Kinrade, Arthur, 10–11
Klaffenbock, Klaus, 166, 175–6, 178–80, 183–4, 186–8, 193
Klankermeier, Max, 22
Konig, 74–5, 83, 92, 95

Lachermair, Gustle, 43, 52
Lambert, Marie, 42
Langman, Harry, 8–10
Langton, Alan, 106–107
Lavorel, Sebastien, 197
Leblonde, Estelle, 197–8
Leeds Mercury, 14
Leek, T., 28
Long, Rick, 133, 140–1, 156–7, 159
Longman, Ernie, 10
Luthringshauser, Heinz, 22, 47, 52, 61, 72, 75, 79

McMillan, Bob, 133, 151
Matchless motorcycles, 24, 46–7
May, Eric, 83
Middlesborough, 2, 58
Mitchell, Andy, 187

Mitchell, Bob, 25–6
Mitchinson, Milton, 79–81
Molyneux, Dave, 112–14, 118, 120, 124–34, 136–51, 155–75, 178, 182–5, 187–92, 196, 200
Molyneux, John, 112, 173
Moore, Roy, 153
Motorcycle News, 100, 134, 145
Murphy, Marty, 107

Neary, Simon, 173, 178
Newton, John, 51
Noll, Wilhelm, 22–4
Norbury, Steve, 152–3, 167
Norton motors, 7, 10, 15, 17–21, 23–4, 26–30, 34–5, 44
Nutt, Les, 20

O'Dell, George, 82–94, 112
Oliver, Eric, 17–19, 23–4, 26–7, 29–30, 32, 35–6, 38–9
Owesle, Horst, 55, 70

Padgett, Clive, 158, 177, 178
Parker, Len, 10–11
Parnell, Scott, 152, 153
Peacock, Eric, 12
Peters, Tom, 190
Potter, Mick, 58

Quarter Bridge, 9, 46–7, 97

RAC, 53
Ramsey, 45–6, 53, 69, 74, 77, 91, 125, 142, 144, 153, 171, 184
Rawlings, Wally, 51
Reeves, Tim, 166–7, 173, 178, 184–5, 188–90, 194–6
Remmert, Karl, 23
Rhencullen, 59, 149, 151
Ried, Josef, 51, 69
Roche, Nick, 115, 117
Rocheleau, Joe and Alma, 76–8
Rowe, Dane, 66–7
Royal sidecars, 22
Rutherford, Johnnie, 101
Rutherford, Peter, 69–70

Saville, Dave, 115–18, 140, 182
Sayle, Dan, 144–6, 164, 169–71, 176–7, 179, 184–5, 193
Schauzu, Seigfried, 22, 54, 58, 61, 67, 69, 72–5, 81–2, 140
Scheidegger, Fritz, 22, 45, 47–8, 50–3, 61
Schleuter, Karl, 45
Schneider, Horst, 54, 58, 67
Schneider, Walter, 23–4, 28, 31–2, 37
Scott motorcycles, 9
Second World War, 17, 19, 21
Seeley, Colin, 22, 46–7, 50, 56–8
Seymaz, 84, 93–4, 99

Sinnott, Steve, 106
Skeels, Mick, 89, 92
Smith, Cyril, 18–20, 25, 29, 34
Smith, Shaun, 104, 109
South Africa, 28, 139
Sprayson, Ken, 57
Spriggs, Brian, 60–3
Steinhausen, Rolf, 74, 89–90, 95, 97
Stoll, Inge, 18–19, 29
Strauss, Hans, 37
Strong, J.R., 14
Sulby, 47, 87, 103–104, 135, 144, 154, 194
Suzuki motors, 86, 106, 114–15, 162–3, 165, 168–9

TT Special, 19, 74
Taylor, Bert, 10–11
Taylor, Jock, 76, 97–101, 103–105, 107, 112, 185
Tinkler brothers, 11
Trachsel, Ernst, 96
Triumph motorcycles, 60, 67, 105
Trollope, Dennis, 76, 99–100
Tucker, George, 9–10, 13
Tuxworth, Neil, 159
Tynwald, 16, 18

URS, 55–7, 61, 68, 70
Union Mills, 46, 52, 57, 110

Vincent HRD motorcycles, 15
Vincent, Chris, 44, 50, 52, 66–7
Vinicombe, Terry, 59

Walker, Graham, 7–9
Wallace, Barry, 101
Watsonian sidecars, 21, 26, 30, 36
Webster, Steve, 105–106, 167
Wells, Dave, 152–4
Wilks, Mark, 195
Willaston Circuit, 16

Windle, Terry, 82–5, 91, 99–100, 108, 197
Winkle, Andy, 152, 153, 166, 176, 188–91, 194
Wise, Pat, 30–3, 35
Wohlgemuth, Alfred, 41
Wynn, Mick, 123

Yamaha motors, 75–6, 78, 81–3, 95, 98–9, 103, 112, 114–15, 119–21, 123, 126, 138
Yorke, Derek, 23–4